# SAMUEL SAYS

## PROPHETIC INSIGHTS FOR THE MODERN AGE

HELEN PORTEOUS

First published in Australia by Aurora House
www.aurorahouse.com.au

This edition published 2024
Copyright © Helen Porteous 2024

Cover design: Donika Mishineva (www.artofdonika.com)
Typesetting and e-book design: Amit Dey (amitdey2528@gmail.com)

ISBN number: 978-1-922913-83-8 (Paperback)

A catalogue record for this
book is available from the
NATIONAL
LIBRARY    National Library of Australia
OF AUSTRALIA

Distributed by: Ingram Content: www.ingramcontent.com
Australia: phone +613 9765 4800 |
email lsiaustralia@ingramcontent.com
Milton Keynes UK: phone +44 (0)845 121 4567 |
email enquiries@ingramcontent.com
La Vergne, TN USA: phone +1 800 509 4156 |
email inquiry@lightningsource.com

# ACKNOWLEDGEMENTS

This book would not have been written, then published, without the efforts and encouragement of two fantastic teams of very patient and hard-working personalities.

Firstly, I thank Samuel and the team of extraordinary Spirit Authors who collectively have an ongoing and immense influence on my life.

Secondly, a big thank you to the publishing team from Aurora House who helped put together a beautiful and interesting book. A talented, professional group of people!

Finally, a big heartfelt thank you to all family, friends, acquaintances, and the little visitors who brought their own magic and learning into my life… the ones with feathers, fur, scales, or leaves. Every encounter and interaction shaped my world view in one way or another.

I am thrilled to offer this book to all readers who still have an active curiosity bump.

✳

**Helen Porteous and Linda Lycett**

Fairy Folk and Other Strange Little Creatures
Fairy Folk and the Magical Helpers
Fairy Folk and Fantastic Friends
Old Man Dots

**Writing as H. M. Porteous:**

Sandy the Flipper Dragon

Titles available from online bookshops

✳

# AUTHOR'S NOTE

If you were unexpectedly visited by a powerful, window-rattling Spirit Personality, how would you react? Would you bolt for the nearest bed and cower under the doona, or be curious enough to stay in the room and see what was about to happen?

And if you did take shelter under the doona, how long would it take before you were brave enough to come out from under it and find out why you were being visited by a messenger from the Realm of Spirit?

This unexpected window-rattling visitation happened to me; and from the start of the energy build-up in the room, I was very curious about what was happening. This startling visitation resulted in an incredible offer being made to me, one that I could accept or not, because it was made very clear from the start that it was entirely my choice.

I have never regretted my immediate decision to accept the chance to work with the team of Spirit Authors, because my life immediately became enriched beyond words.

Helen Porteous

# CONTENTS

# PREFACE

The energy in the large, glass-walled room was highly charged. It was absolutely electric! Every individual hair on my body was standing on end and there was a tangible feel of wonder, laughter, and angelic power in the room. Because of the unusual circumstances in my personal life at this time, I had decided to learn the techniques needed to do automatic writing. In the previous weeks I had made several minor attempts, but the results were non-legible scrawls on the paper. This specific Thursday evening, I was visiting with a friend who offered to give me advice on the techniques she had used, and also to give suggestions on how to allow events to unfold without putting my expectations into the mix. This evening's attempt was about to become totally different from all previous attempts.

I started the exercise by using a pendulum to elicit 'yes', 'no', or 'maybe' answers and initially it seemed to be working well. But this gentle activity was about to change. The room became even more strongly energised than it was before, and it felt like a bow wave of wonderful energy was filling the large room. The heavy quartz pendulum I was holding began to dance; it swung and looped in patterns with gravity defying and joyful abandon. And I mean gravity defying because at one time the pendulum was upright on the cotton cord and stayed in that position until I made an inane comment about the impossibility of this happening. The room was filled with love, laughter, and wonderful flashing lights and I knew that something wonderful and eventful was happening and that I was a very lucky lady to be experiencing this uplifting energy.

At this stage, my friend suggested that maybe it was time to put the pendulum down and pick up the pen, so the pendulum was put to one side, and the pen picked up and poised lightly on a page of my journal. The 'yes' and 'no' answers to our questions were now being written with strength and surety. The writing was still a bit wobbly but legible enough. And at the same time the room became even more electrified and filled with joyous, sparkling energy.

In response to some questions, hard raps were heard on the glass doors that were across the other side of the large room. The huge windows were rattling, and the doors were shaking. There was a feeling of everything being 'right' in the world and as it was meant to be.

I began by asking how we were meant to proceed and the pen, which was held loosely in my hand, began to move freely across the paper. It began to slowly write a sentence on the open page and in response to my question, the words, "Spirits dictate essay on spiritualism" were written.

This became the opening sentence of a most extraordinary communication. The writing started out spidery and in places difficult to understand. A few words were repeated for me, and some I have not deciphered all these years later. I am recording the essay exactly as it came onto the paper that extraordinary evening and I have indicated the unknown words. At 9.30 p.m., this essay was written and it changed my life for the better.

The place of work is everywhere. How do we feel about it all? What is the essence of the whole exercise? What do you want to say or learn? Do the [unknown word] wasteful times, may be small-minded people so that small-minded people can understand? Is this what you want to see? No, not a waste of time; no, not at all. It is all important, so be patient. Small things make a major difference. Wellness is a state of mind so must be allowed to develop at the most [marked?] place and time.

What's the meaning of all the words that have been written most of the time? When the Spirits call the shots, most of the words must be well-written news. With all that has been done, it must be nitty gritty and profound at all times. How will all the people waste moments all the while? What is the most wanted message that most will want to know? How will we tell when the message is the correct one when your world is in the worst worries imaginable? Your day of troubles is not so far away.

*At this stage I could feel heavy zipping and zapping all over my body. The room remained intensely electrified and uplifting, and the writing on the paper was quickly becoming stronger and easier to 'hear' as well as record.*

Yes, it will not be so far away that the time to start learning is here.

So, when we talk is near in time. What will be the outcome of all the books and letters that have been mustered at this time? When will news come out into the open and shake the wowsers out of their dogma and open their eyes? When will the news be mostly needed? Always! Many will be gone, and all the news will mostly mean nothing to the masses at this time of the mourning.

How will the masses be able to cope without the news of deliverance and hope? Who will be the lucky ones and who will be the worried ones when the sadness is at the peak of times? How will they be able to say they are delivered when they don't know what to say and feel about all things? What do the people believe? That they will not be able to understand? The news and the promise of another reality that seems so far away and hard to understand? So, what is the answer to all this? What is the final solution? It is the teaching of the news to the masses and the HOPE of all the good things to come. The Almighty Gods are about and plentiful with the LOVE OF ALL THINGS.

*This is signed with a flowing letter—sort of an 'L' or a loose 'S' shape.*

*Well, that was the end of the essay. The above version is basically how the punctuation and composition appeared, and it clearly shows how the language of the first contact was not a modern way of expression. The energetic electricity remained extremely strong the whole time. When I asked who was writing these words, the name "Samuel" was written. As this name emerged onto the page all the windows and doors in the large room rattled and shook; the energy was absolutely stunning. I asked if Samuel was one of my 'guides' and the answer came.*

No, Samuel is a Speaker, is the Teacher and Communicator.

*The glass windows and doors still thrummed with energy, so I got up and walked towards the window and double glass door. As I neared them, I felt as though I was stepping into an electric current of joy, goodwill, and celebration. I was laughing and thoroughly enjoying the experience.*

*My friend was quietly watching but not involved in the activity. Even so, she could feel the energy and hear the windows and doors rattle. She said right from the start that what was happening was meant for me personally. The above essay arrived out of the blue; it was totally unexpected because all I had been trying to do was some legible automatic writing.*

*At this stage we stopped for a break, and that gave us time to formulate pertinent questions. The information kept coming in further writing sessions that evening and it was told to me that I would be helping to co-write books with Spirit Personalities if I accepted the offer to do so, and*

*That all things will flow easily, and the means will be provided to enable me to carry on with the written words at all times.*

*From this night onwards, I began to keep journals of all the spirit communications I received, recording the questions and answers, visions, and impressions. As this intricate and comprehensive communication progressed, my intuitive abilities strengthened and expanded as a whole range of clairvoyant skills emerged during the daily activities—such as knowing when things were about to happen, sensing distant family issues, being able to visualise where misplaced items were, and so on. Coincidences became the norm and it became second nature for me to connect the dots to work out messages, or the reasons why events happened as they did.*

*I had embarked on a crash course of remembering again the innate and intuitive skills that had been forgotten or poorly used until now. My numerous unseen Spirit Helpers, Guides, Teachers, and Friends kept gently pushing and encouraging me to use my curiosity as a tool to delve into new levels of energetic work.*

*In the following years, Samuel took a back seat while other mentors in Spirit helped prepare the way for his communications. The references to Samuel popped up now and again in the daily journals so I knew somewhere up there, Samuel was watching and waiting.*

*The references below came over a four-year time frame and always involved a subtle educational input of some kind.*

There are other things you need to do first, not with the meditation, but with Samuel. Samuel will lead you on a beautiful guided tour so to speak, and reacquaint you with your ancient knowledge.

Your goals have been hinted at, we have a great deal of writing to be done, and with the Angel Samuel this will be a major task for you. Samuel is a high-vibrational Essence and will bring many gifts in his Light.

Allow the pen to flow. It is good to see the words come flowing onto the page. This is the feeling you will feel when Samuel begins his work. The pen will have energy of its own and the words will appear with a glorious glee.

No rest, Samuel is coming.

You have been trying to work out who Samuel is. We say this, Samuel in your book and in historical terms would be classed as an Archangel, one of the seven who sits beside the Lord. Other names are immaterial but are there. He is a Blessed One and has the power of love so strong that the teachings from this Great Soul need the students to understand the connections and the emotions of the word. Samuel is a Mighty Lord of the Universe, and the power of creation is immense. As a group of Spirit Helpers, we are greatly privileged to be doing this work with, and for, the Blessed One.

He sits with the Blessed Ones and the love is profound. And again, we say to you Ahale, you are not forgotten, all is being watched with great interest, and what you would call suggestions are handed down the line so to speak.

There indeed will be heavy responsibilities, but it will be your choice to stand and shoulder them. For as you do this, you will be setting up a strong base or foundation for your work with Samuel. We have not forgotten about this and you have not either.

*There was a real sense of fun and humour about the room when this was written, and by the way, Ahale is one of the names the Spirit Team say they know me by.*

When Samuel begins you will begin a more balanced writing regime and a timetable will develop that allows the best use of time.

It is quite an interesting subject, to see how each individual handles energy communication. And Samuel, in all probability, will speak of this aspect also.

You understand this on a shallow level yet. You feel the depths and know it is there, but until you acknowledge the new ground you are preparing and the new way of teaching that Samuel is interested in, you have not yet begun to understand the unlimited depths of what we speak.

There will be no thunderclaps, but you will see that all events will flow in a nice, coincidental way so when the beloved Samuel begins it will feel like a wonderful and timely continuation.

The words will be able to explain the unexplainable in terms that the average person can understand. This will be the 'hook', and so the influence of the contact with Samuel will have a profound and continuing effect. This is how it is.

Samuel is close, do you feel this?

*In April, Samuel himself spoke briefly. I say spoke, but his is really a multi-layered communication.*

Listen, you have waited to go 'upwards', so hello now. Open up the heart, Ahale, be ready for now and be ready for a long, mighty task to begin. Just wait; you will know when to start.

*When Samuel wrote this, there seemed to be very strong energy with a lot of laughter and good humour about, and this cheered me up at the time. This was Samuel's second contact, and the contact energy was unmistakable.*

Now, as for Samuel's writing, never fear—it will happen. You were simply given a long warning that enabled you to begin your learning and journey of self-exploration. The writing has been steadily prepared for and it requires one more issue to be dealt with before the decks are cleared.

*I had just reread the original essay from three years earlier.*

The energy of the earlier writing is strong and connected to Samuel. We have already said that He has heard the bowl singing. He is close, closer than you realise, dear one. Closer than you realise.

*I frequently play a small Tibetan singing bowl before meditation.*

Do not worry how the words get written. Simply write them and we will see what comes forth. No matter how or why, it will be an interesting exercise for you. Now the language will always be kept simple. Both Samuel and Mary will do this. Mary will have her say and stay with you. Samuel will also have his say. A busy time indeed.

*A very cheeky sense of humour came through and plopped with glee into these words. And the reference to 'Mary' is about another Spirit author I have been told is waiting in the queue.*

*Samuel himself eventually wrote.*

We are near. Do not be afraid of goodbyes. We are close; please know this. Do not worry about the writing. Tonnes will be done in another place.

*This reference to another place was of great interest. At this specific time, I was unable to find anywhere I could afford to rent, so I was unsettled and extremely stressed about my living situation. Despite my predicament, the humorous feeling wrapping around and infused within the following words was so strong that I ended up laughing and feeling that everything was alright in my world.*

Want a cuddle? Old memories! Everything will be put into perspective.

Plan your day and stick to a schedule if you feel you need to. However, spontaneity has its own rewards.

*This particular morning, the familiar word flow seemed to change. The words flowed onto the page in a different writing style, and then a wavy line appeared. The change in the energy of the writing was tangible; it was not a subtle wispy sensation but an overt and powerful one.*

Wave upon wave of energy, energy, energy, wave upon wave. Put on the oilskins and be prepared to stand against these waves of energy that will buffet your space. Stand proudly against it all and come out in the end, the victor against chaos. The chaos of man, not God.

I am Samuel, dear one, the One you have been waiting to hear from. We will speak time and time again of things that glitter in the sunshine and things that go bump in the night. Let the wave be my signature, so that you know who speaks with you. You are most beloved of God and will be a proud Warrior of Light once again. You talk to us even more than you realise, dear one. When you sleep you are busy indeed.

For now, continue with your scheduled works. I will begin my book in the time of closeness. The signature will be the clue for you...which journal to take out from the closet and let the moths fly free.

We will do a parallel series to the blessed Mary, a parallel series, not the same; we come from a different angle. You will have eight books all up from this double series. This is a powerful unifier for all; indeed, it is infinity, is it not? In the future close to you, light the incense, take up a pen, and label a journal:

## "SAMUEL SAYS"

*These are examples of the comments about Samuel that spanned over four years. One time, I heard a voice calling my name and I raced to the door because the sound seemed to come from that direction. No one was there.*

*The voice sounded as though it came from a vast distance; it sounded androgynous, with a foreign or alien lisp. This was a voice I had not heard physically before. So, I asked who had called my name.*

Samuel. He has shown you a focus of his energy. He was trying to wake you up [it was 7.15 a.m.] and you have actually described the voice fairly well. Reread what you previously wrote. There was immense power behind the sound. You will hear this voice again and again and again.

*By this time, I had many questions about this 'biblical' Samuel and wanted to find out who He was, so I borrowed a Bible and other biblical books and tried to find a Samuel who had been in Genesis. Samuel is not mentioned in the Bible until the Book of Samuel, so I questioned this anomaly. I am not familiar with the biblical set up, so did I miss a reference?*

Samuel is amused with your reading; he smiles on you and your bible reading. He is in Genesis and all other biblical books. And so are you and everyone else. What does Genesis mean?

*The beginning... the origin.*

Yes, and take it to mean exactly that.

*This was an interesting time for me because by now, I was busy recording a series of books with the beloved Mary, who introduced herself four years after the initial offer to co-write books was made. We had a regular daily schedule for the dictation and recording of her words.*

*When Samuel began his dictation there was quite a length of time when both Mary and Samuel would dictate their words on the same day but at their selected time. It didn't feel strange to me because they were both so different in how they expressed the words, and it was easy for me to know who was in the room, so to speak, because of the powerful sense of presence both had.*

*Also, I had already been told Mary's writing would be for beginners in their search for answers on metaphysical knowledge and to liken her words to kindergarten teachings, and Samuel's words would reinforce and expand on what she wrote, so to liken his words to first grade teachings, and so it all seemed logical and not out of context.*

*Between all their words and insights, a smooth and interesting learning stimulus had been planned, and over time words emerged offering new insights to anyone interested. I would be ready and waiting at the desk at the chosen time and usually record for an hour with Mary, or until her session was finished.*

*I would have a break, then the unmistakeable Samuel energy would flood the room, and away we would go, with me scrambling to record all the words that came before me. I also tried to record how it all felt, because Samuel was such a powerhouse of energy.*

*The interaction between both authors continued until the Mary series finished. Within weeks of this happening, Samuel suggested it was time to exclusively begin his scheduled writings. And so, we began.*

# INTRODUCTION

*S amuel dictated this introduction. Since our window-rattling first contact, I had undergone a long and intense time of learning, and it felt amazing to be getting started on something that was planned so long ago.*

This is an introductory talk, dear one. We watch and help in all ways we can: you do well and will do better as time goes by. This is a brief hello to introduce myself and others. I am in your Bible. I am in Genesis as Samuel the Prophet. I have been many identities, but this one as Samuel will connect with your energy well.

The Prophet began in the early part of the Bible story and was a forerunner of the events that followed down the time stream. The Earth is in a state of change in both physical and non-physical ways. A huge stellar shift is happening, and the cosmic forces play a major part in how, why, and when things eventuate. The Pole star has resurfaced in your life at this point of the 'now' for a very valid reason.

You have walked through the energy of this star gate many times. You understand the feeling of the vibrational shifts around you, and you will not be spooked by what is to happen. Dear one, you are a part of a large, large group of souls who are diligently reaching out and connecting to the Source and then teaching this knowledge to the people who want to hear. A vast group indeed!

The Light Workers of your World are working well with the Light Workers of our Worlds. Down through the Ages a good line of communication has been formed, and this connection will strengthen dramatically in the coming times. This teaching is of importance for the survival of the integrity of the Plan.

The Plan is a blueprint of the unlimited Universe, and as a working model, many movements are constantly in motion. This is a fact. The Universe breathes in, and it breathes out.

As each individual Soul travels through the different lifetimes and fully experiences these realities, it also goes through many of these breaths. It is the rhythmic in and the rhythmic out, the dancing in and the dancing out. Every one of you has experienced this. Now, this is a time of the in breath, of drawing in the Creator's Breath.

The Energy is immense and can be felt by all peoples, whether they are attuned to it or not. Some will brush this energy aside as being a nuisance thought or feeling that comes unbidden into the back of their mind. Others will be curious but not curious enough to do anything about it. Others will feel it and know what it represents, and they will joyfully embrace this Energy. The people who do this are the Light Workers, the Guardians, the Keepers, and the Storytellers of the Myths of Creation. This is their time, and so we begin the work: the teaching and the understanding of the Breath of God.

Many, many different names and identities have my many selves experienced, with all individual identities being bountiful and fruitful cycles in the great Creative experience. We collectively see the sum total of what is to happen; we see the changes, the hopes, and the aspirations of Souls. What a beautiful existence is possible for everyone!

Now, at this point we will not tell everything about me; it is more about you and everyone else. You each have the chance to do great teaching work at this time. And you each have known this was to happen before you became the 'you' in this life, and it is now a part of a larger plan of the Group you are working within.

Think of it like this, you are on a group field trip and are helping to set the scene for the Teacher of Teachers to be able to arrive in a fertile field. Your Group has a powerful message of Hope and Love.

The beloved Mary has begun her work with you, Ahale.

She comes down to the everyday level to explain to the unknowing ones some Universal insights. She works as an introduction for our work. It has all been planned and the work has begun and will continue with you or with others. You are a part of this team because messages from the Creator can be told in many ways. The written word is one way only.

Some unusual events will occur that will bring people's awareness to these words. Believe in what is happening, for it is happening. Do not ever doubt this message coming to you now because even your dreams are telling you that you are involved in the 'Star and Cosmic' business.

Dear lady, never doubt what you do. It is very valid work and will be seen to be such in the future of your time. You are a capable team member and have proved your worth over many turns of the Wheel. You may have wandered a little, but you never forgot the underlying feelings. This is why you feel comfortable with what we do. You are in familiar territory. Between us we have a series of eight works to be done. Put a candle in the window as a symbolic gesture of welcoming a new dawn of insights and information, and it will act as a focal point for everyone!

*Here, Samuel must have seen my concern about not only the true scope of what was being suggested, but also the possibility of these words being published at some time in the future. Since the first contact, I knew that books were in the pipeline, but to have them becoming real is a different situation.*

*A much later update: by the time Mary had finished her dictating, there were twelve smaller books that I eventually combined in four volumes, and Samuel wrote four additional books, so there was a total of eight books in this combined series. The lessons and insights flowed seamlessly from the basic introduction through to the next level of information.*

Now we will need some explanation of what it is we try to accomplish. We aim to explain the hidden realms in terms of what and how everyday experiences impinge on each person. We will leave the in-depth and sometimes weird theories for another time and just keep concentrating on how a person reacts to everyday life experiences.

You are a mote of dust on a windowpane. You are at the surface or interface of a beautiful vista, or maybe an unlimited panoramic view. Yet because your attention is directed to being a dust mote, you do not fully understand that you are allowed to lift this focus from the dust mote level and see the bigger picture around you.

The dust mote is allowed to see through the glass, yet in most cases the thought will not enter its mind that this action is even an option. When all the other dust motes are sitting on the glass looking content, why would you want to be the dust mote that disturbs the peace by doing something different?

You can see through the glass. It is simply where the focus goes to that controls the viewing area.

Do you want to be a dust mote? If you, as a dust mote, do not want to stay silently stuck on a windowpane, then simply decide that it is time to learn more. Learn more about where you are sitting, more about your fellow dust motes, more about the opaqueness or transparency of the glass. You can choose.

Of course, you and all others are not dust motes. You are wonderful, complex entities with unlimited windows and pathways linked to even more windows and pathways. You are a Child of God in human form. Let me also say the dust mote is also a Child of God but will experience its God connection in another aspect of reality. You have the blueprint of the Universe already embedded in your psyche and all it needs is your openness and curiosity to be given unrestricted freedom to allow this knowledge to spontaneously emerge.

Because of cultural or family conditioning you may feel that to allow your curiosity to free range may be a bit presumptuous. You also may feel that you are comfortable enough as you are and you don't want to rock the boat.

Sorry, but that is not an excuse, an alibi, or a valid reason to hide behind the laziness...the laziness of the thinking, emotional, and spiritual processes. To rock any boat means that you have to make movements that unsettle the status quo, or the balance, and any harmony you think you have.

Let me say to you, one and all, if you are an active, participating human at this time in the turn of the Cosmic Wheel and you do not want to rock the boat, then it will be done for you.

This is no threat or idle talk. The basic tenet of becoming human is to experience, learn, and understand how to use and create with vibrational energy. The reasons coupled to the existence of your physical experiences suggests that you need to remember and relearn the underlying reasons why energy imbalances can rock the boat.

You need to understand how the unseen forces of energy work and how you may react to them as an energy gestalt in your own right. You need to know how to rock the boat and how to compensate by balancing the opposing vibrational forces. As I have said, if you, one and all, in this turn of the Cosmic Wheel, do not desire to learn about energy connections and balancing, you will as a sentient race be forced to respond to stimuli at a time not of your choosing.

*This is hard to describe, but there was a lovely sense of humour and at the same time a seriousness around these words. Humour mixed with seriousness is an odd mix and doesn't always blend smoothly, but in this case, it blended beautifully and it all felt so right to me.*

There is always movement, always growth, and never stillness. You have been warned, so allow the cobwebs to drift away from your thoughts and as with our individualistic dust mote, dare to look through the glass to the Universal visions beyond.

Now, to do this a person needs to let go of any self-taught limits. Everyone has their own agenda or comfort zones that they do not want to step away from despite what happens to them. But think on this, does your comfort zone still comfort you? Does your comfort zone still have solid walls that keep out the woes and troubles of the world? Is your comfort zone being rocked?

Are you coping with all the ongoing emotional upsets, and is the media reporting of the world's disasters bothering you in any way? Does unsettling news or actions of a family member upset you? Is your comfort zone still strong? Or is it cracking and allowing glimpses of a terrifying unknown to peek through?

Many events are happening in your world right now that will crumble little pieces away from your walled comfort zone despite all your attempts at patching the cracks. If these global events do not touch you in any way, then your inner self will find a way to force you to see what is happening and make you aware of the shifting horizons for mankind because these new horizons are coming at mankind in wave after wave of change. In one way or another, each and every soul is being tested, pushed, and encouraged to see the bigger cosmic picture.

*Humorous imagery kept flowing on my inner movie screen, and it was all rather fun because Samuel was talking about a very serious subject here, but he was showing it to me how a newly individualistic and enlightened dust mote might see it.*

Will you be like a blind dust mote and cling to the familiar glass, or will you be an enlightened dust mote and turn your focus to this bigger picture? It's your choice, but please understand this; your time of choosing is becoming shorter and you really need to see what is happening about you and react in a balanced and informative way.

Are you a frightened little mote or a mote of courage and curiosity? And remember, it is always, always your choice to be whatever you wish. I hope for you the ability to see the bigger picture in all its splendour, in all the colours, feelings, insights, communications, and friendships, and have these all wrapped within a cocoon of unconditional Love.

The time to choose your destiny is now, not tomorrow or next week or even next year. It is time to open up the curiosity box, let all the senses blossom into magnificence, and stimulate courage to help balance the books of creation. Love is the energy that balances these books. Does your wall of comfort keep love in or keep it out? Hmm?

*The next few paragraphs were not written specifically by Samuel for the manuscript, because they were written in my personal journal. The words have a bearing on the current subjects and biblical characters, and I am putting them in as extra insight on some of the concepts just mentioned. These extra writings and information snippets in my daily journal often explain in greater detail, or from another angle, some aspects of what Samuel is writing about in his manuscript. Or they are Samuel's response to a question I have asked.*

Harken the advice about going within. Now, 'time' is a strange thing in your terms...a time to do this or to do that. We see it more as a nexus working to its capacity.

*The names mentioned below have been mentioned before in the daily writings.*

Jacob is not as he is written about in your Bible; the same situation applies to him as to the beloved Mary. He quietly and effectively goes about the Creator's work without the fanfare of trumpets and is a very powerful and wonderful Teacher. You don't need to go and research this because the knowledge is within. Be still and allow it to flow into your conscious mind, because the historical times, as recorded, have no meaning as you well know.

It doesn't matter if Samuel the Prophet knew Jacob, Moses, Jezus, Mary Magdalene, or anyone named in the early stories. All were, and still are, working together at all times. One or another may have lived on Earth at any given time, but a continuing link connects strongly to all personalities at all times.

Many souls have worked together time after time after time to bring enlightenment to themselves and others. When do you think all this started? Halfway through the story? You were all there from before the beginning, from the original moment of the creation of mankind.

You are all in Genesis; you were all there before the beginning.

And now it is another time and age for great teachings to be done before the vibrational change alters your world. And so, you all come together as before, as before.

But the dawn will have a surprise for mankind. As the Light brightens and the shadows fall away, the view will be quite unusual in some parts of the world. Little pockets of brilliant illumination will shine like beacons in the dark. This Light will draw others to its comfort and warmth, and for the Light to bloom to its fullest potential the individual and group flames need to be burning pure and strong, sturdily upright, and not fluttering about in the wind.

Testing times for each individual are activated for very valid reasons. As each person clears away the dross, the inner Light shines clearer and stronger. And dear one, when a group of such Light Workers come together as one, the Light is intensified.

Even from our side of reality, we see these Lights as beacons of hope and as God's Energy at work. Special characters and personalities are needed on all levels of reality, with all working together. A special team is needed for the special work to be done. We in the Spiritual Realms are preparing, just as each individual in your physical reality is preparing.

Samuel the Prophet is one of my identities and that is the one I will use for this exercise. The biblical names coming into human awareness at this time through intuitive books, visions, dreams, healings, and in uncounted numbers is almost an unplanned occurrence.

Many of us come back into humanity's awareness in times of need and down through history; groups of trouble-shooters have gathered, are gathering, and will continue to gather, to teach others and to again experience for themselves the magic of the Creator's Energy in action.

Many such trouble-shooters are still gathering to help and experience the vibrational birth of human consciousness into the New Dawn. So yes, many who come will have biblical names. That is alright. It is something to be used as a focal point because it is easier to bring to mind an artist's impression of an old man called 'Samuel the Prophet' sitting on a park bench, with a long white beard and wearing long white robes and leather sandals, than it is to focus on a misty cloud of a nebulous nothing.

Therefore, using biblical personalities and names can be useful. Get the working boots on, beloved daughter. You go to work on ignorance and intolerance. You go to war for the Light. The day of dawning of the New Light is here. The ones who are awake early are the ones who will see the beautiful Light rise gently over the horizon.

*As I read through the above words all these years later, I get very emotional. It is like my heart is filling with joy and wonder at the scope and in-depth interaction that Samuel speaks of. I am quite teary.*

# 1

# GENESIS, STAR LANES, AND
# HEAVENLY MESSAGES

Do we actually know when the beginning began? At what point in the long, distant past did it actually happen? If you are following a specific tick-tock time listed in the science or history books, you need to know how incorrect this listing is.

The beginning is in your present time, now, and will continue to be so. Do you think the stories in the known holy books tell the beginning of everything? Do the Genesis and Creation stories tell of the making of you? No.

The word genesis means at the beginning. It means that the symbolic awareness of mankind was triggered into action in a certain way at this time. You were not made or manufactured as an entity or as a species at this time, but the awareness of who and what you are began to be known. And this is the story I give to you.

You. Your Soul Energy is not a new energy that sprang from the Garden of Eden. You were a viable, aware, and sentient being long, long, long before you came 'down' to the

Earth. You are a Star Soul. You have knowledge of the Stars in a very complete and complex way, and not as an astrologer who studies the distant galaxies through a telescope either small or large.

You know these places because you have lived, existed, and still exist as a Star Soul. You have travelled the Star lanes, and they are all familiar to you. Do you not feel this when you sometimes go outside and look at the magical night sky? Do you feel a tightening and stirring of your emotions? Does an odd feeling that is hard to define sweep through you? Do you connect in some way, with the majestic feel of the heavens? Of course, you do; you have travelled these lanes and this memory is still encoded deeply into your cellular matrix... your Soul Essence.

Put aside disbelief at these words for a moment and allow your imagination to let loose and fly. Does it feel possible that you have lived amongst the distant galaxies or some unknown reality at some time or another, in some form or another? Remember, you are a Spiritual being who knows no boundaries, because you are an entity who can leap the tallest mountain in a single leap and who can see all things, past, present, future, all at the same time.

You do not remember this? Then dear, doubting person, imagine that this is so, set your imagination free, and allow it to soar without restrictions, and then allow it to take you out into the galaxies and roam freely along the Star lanes. You will see familiar markers and signposts scattered here and there. Mind you, they may not look exactly like the signs you have here on Earth, ones with arrows pointing to this or that, and some with names of places with population totals as well. These Star lane signposts will be signposts of 'knowing' and 'feeling' and not solid substances of wood, stone, or anything else physical.

*There is a sort of Superman/Superwoman humour whizzing around the page. I think the comical bit here is that you don't have to imagine or pretend anything; you just have to remember forgotten knowledge.*

Some readers will feel an affinity for different Star groups and not really know why this is so. Maybe the name of the constellations will feel sweet on the tongue, or the patterns made by the stars themselves will draw your heart and eye to them. Also, any intuitive spiritual numbers, musical sounds and inputs from all other sources you feel affinity with, whether they be from Star lanes, universes stacked within universes, or a full moon glowing on a warm summer night, will resonate in your soul. Little twitches of awareness and closeness will pop into your thoughts without you consciously knowing where they originate from. They come from the depths of your ancient memories, and is a natural progression of knowing who and what you are: a Star Soul experiencing a brief time as a student of physical creativity!

The genesis began before the described biblical stories, this you now know. You are a Space Soul, a Star Soul, a Universal Soul, an Everything Soul, and the name is almost immaterial, so take your pick of which you prefer to use right now, just remember to accept no limitations with whatever name you choose to identify with. The biblical stories tell of a symbolic beginning of this adventure on Earth, the beginning of the full creative understanding of this physical schoolroom called life.

The schoolroom description is apt because as the Star Soul sent tendrils of itself into the physical level, it also sent parameters and a syllabus of lessons to be learnt. The guidelines suggested were programmed then offered at a level of simplicity and complexity that would be understandable to all the souls who chose to experience this creativity. And what better way of doing this than to incorporate guidelines and knowledge into stories?

Stories and parables can be entertaining and educational at the same time, so stories of Creation were written with this in mind. And in this manner began the teaching and enlightenment of mankind. There are nuggets of truth scattered amongst the holy books and cultural mythology. Read them and listen to them with an open heart, because the Star connection is there to be noted. This is not just the rambling thoughts of an old, old soul. The ideas so expressed come not from my imagination but from the Creative Universe itself.

*This was so much fun for me to write down because so much humour and good will kept floating about as all this was being recorded. These lovely humorous feelings were palpable to me as I sat writing this down; for example, the 'old, old soul' quote made me laugh because of the way Samuel put the words down. Wry, comical, wistful, cheeky but powerful, and emotional all mixed in together.*

So, do you feel you still live only in a fleshy body that walks on the Earth's surface, and that this body defines the limit of 'you'? Do you ever wonder exactly how you came into being in the first place? Exactly what it is that the unused part of your brain is supposed to do? Exactly who are you and what are you supposed to be doing? Even children in their sweet and total innocence ask questions they want to have answered.

Can you answer these childish questions about where we come from, why we look like we do? Why? Why? Why? Give yourself permission to find out these answers by opening up to your own curiosity, and look through, under, inside, outside, and over established Creation theories.

Look to see if you can find the grains of truth hidden amongst the stories and legends, and if you do find some, hopefully they will bring enrichment and excited understanding into your life. To look honestly and without limitations is to allow your Spirit freedom to roam without restriction.

Do not be afraid to question holy books. Always look to see what the words are saying underneath, and discover what is deeply encoded into the manuscripts for the people who seek the truth to find. Look at the Garden of Eden story with new eyes, new ears, and new intuitions. The beginning of what? What are the symbolic messages saying exactly? Go that next step deeper and see what is being taught beneath the words. Yes indeed.

All creation is a beginning of change of some type or another, a making, a breaking, and an alteration of energy. Therefore, it stands to reason that the biblical stories of Creation are symbolic stories of change and new awareness—changes in a long, long, eternal line of changes.

But you need to look further back along the line so that you can sense the continuity of your Soul Energy. Look to see further back into the earlier changes that you, as a Star Soul, have known. Do not limit your focus to a tiny part of the whole, because you deserve better than that. You deserve to see more of the bigger picture, the bigger cosmic picture. Are you game enough to go out into the night and remember?

*The session finished, but Samuel often has more to say that is not specifically book dictation. The given advice: 'Chapter one still has more to go, and the book dictation will resume in another place.'*

*Little did I know, but I was about to move to another place to live.*

*He said to go outside and look for the rainbow, and sure enough a rainbow was visible, and as I watched, the rain began easing.*

*As Samuel is dictating, whether it is for his manuscript or words of advice written in my journal… for want of a more descriptive word… the energy in the room is beautiful. A strong presence can be felt, and when the session ends there is a palpable feeling of a loss of close contact.*

*The following is an extra dictation that came, and I was not sure at the start whether it was book dictation or not, because it was recorded at a different time of the day from the regular contact slot. I will include it in this chapter mainly because of the timing aspect.*

Good evening, dearest daughter, know this is a part of book dictation. It will not be for a specific place as yet, and this placing will be sorted out at a later time. Uncountable are the souls who have lived many lives—many, many lives—and have trouble understanding the concepts of why this has been so.

Many of these lives have been lived in a manner of 'marching on the spot', neither advancing nor retreating, just holding onto the status quo. These souls who are now living in this exciting day and age may need to be given a little push or shunt to help them move away from the well trampled spot.

Now, these lives can be good lives, with the people judged to be worthy souls who do good deeds, or maybe they are judged as good people who seem to be drifting along and never exerting themselves by doing or experiencing much of anything new. I speak of the inherent possibilities of wisdom learning that are consciously bypassed, not noticed, or deliberately ignored.

These are aspects of learning, and the understanding of these lessons that has been set forth at the beginning of each incarnation. I speak of the souls who miss the opportunities to become one with the One. There are a surprising number of you out there in the big, wide world who have not taken advantage of the opportunities presented to you. You have allowed these chances to slide on by, and you have chosen not to allow your feet to get wet, or your breath to quicken with excitement. You have not wanted to be bothered.

I will tell you in stark black and white words. You are heading into the time when you will be forcefully bothered. The times of mankind are in flux, and no one will be left unbothered and allowed to sit undisturbed in a corner. You will not be able to hide, and you will not be able to sit with your face hidden under a blanket of indifference.

You will be seen by the Spirits of the Creators, the Spirits of God, and the Spirits of You, and you will, without any preliminary social chitchat have any camouflage ripped away from your space. This will leave you unprotected and wide open to the energy vibrations of the rising tide. You will be forced to acknowledge that a new day for mankind is dawning and you are included in this changing time, ready or not.

And so, I say to you there is no point in hiding or pretending you don't know what is happening. There is already a surge of knowledge, a strong surge of spiritual teachings sweeping around the world. The teachings about changes for mankind are abundant, and there will be no person living who will not be touched and invigorated in some way or another by this universal knowledge.

You may be a lonely hermit living in a desert area, totally isolated from other human contact, yet even you will be given teachings, signs, symbols, dream messages, elemental interaction, and acknowledgements in a very personal way. You will still be tuning into the rising energetic dance.

At first you may not know what it is that you are feeling and sensing, but your attention may be drawn to something as simple as a shimmering colour that appears over the bare earth, or something you see that is a little out of the usual, yet in an odd way feels to be alright. It feels as though this shimmering colour fits into the day.

Or it may be a visionary effect with unusual dancing lights appearing before your eyes and again, they feel non-threatening despite the strangeness and suddenness of how they appeared. You know there is something unusual and important going on. Many large and many little ways will be found to drag even the most reluctant hermit into understanding that the world is moving into a newness not seen before.

Now, hermits are solitary people, usually shunning human contact as much as possible, but you may also be called a hermit even when living amongst the multitude if you shut yourself off from contact with others by building barriers between yourself and everyone else. If this is the case, then you will have your barriers shattered and battered aside, because each and every individual will be given the choice of reaching forward towards the New Dimension, the new level of Godly connections.

You will be given the choice and all efforts will be expended to encourage you to open up to this beautiful experience. If you choose to ignore all help and all warnings, dear one, you will be, without hesitation, left behind to become the unenlightened blob you have chosen to be.

All help will be offered, but there is a deadline looming in mankind's future and it's rapidly heading your way. You are being given an opportunity to be a shining part of the Universal team and I, known as Samuel the Prophet, dare you to step outside your comfort zone and open up to change.

Mind you, even if you decide to be like a lump on a log and not exert yourself at all, you will not be shrivelled into a little ball of nothingness, because you still have the matrix of Divine Energy as the building block for your lumpiness on a log. But you will be a dull little vibrational lump on the log, a gloomy lump who will know that he or she has missed the boat, and you will know that you have been left behind and there is little you can do to change the situation.

I speak the words of a Prophet. It has been my job for time uncounted to help prepare the way for uplifting change, to help prepare the way for new levels of existence, and to assist in any way that I am able to do so. Many times, I have been told of my forthright manner of speaking, but why do I need to change this? Because it is a manner of speaking that allows little room for misinterpretation. Never will you be able to say that you have read my words and did not understand their meaning.

It does not matter what language you speak or read, and it doesn't matter where on this beautiful planet you come from because you will be receiving messages from one source or another that say to you: 'Wake up! A New Dawn is here, awaken and join with the Light' and the messages will be tailored to your exact needs and level of awareness. Because this is what your Spirit Helpers, your Guides, your Angels do for, and with, you. They see in what way you can be reached or touched by the incoming messages, and so your individual needs will always be addressed. You will have no excuses if you ignore the Godly messages. The Creator's voice comes to you in unlimited ways and this voice is all around you.

Wake up, dear readers, your time of choosing is here. Listen to the words of the Creator or be in danger of being left in misery and in a coldness and emptiness of your own choosing. I will speak more of these messages that are about you, simply to show that what I say is indeed the truth. Never let it be said that the message I give is unclear.

*There was a hiatus of five months after the words above were dictated. There were stretches of time when other major things were happening in my life, and these usually involved steep learning curves of one sort or another. Samuel readily gave me personal advice on everything and anything, and the thoughts and suggestions were always spot on and accepted by me in the spirit they were meant.*

*Therefore, the subject matter is not quite in line with the last dictated paragraphs, but in many convoluted ways it is connected to them.*

You have to be in tune with your own feelings, dearest daughter. Listen to 'you' instead of listening to others. Empathy can be turned inwards as well as outwards. You need to do this in a more honest way. Oh, you know I speak truly, you know this. The obstacles in your life are clearing gradually, and it will soon be a 'go' for our work. It is enjoyable watching these obstacles slide into the mist and the biggest emotional one of all has been allowed to disperse.

This has been hard for you to do because these obstacles have been acting as an anchor or attachment to your past. You have now symbolically cut the ties that bind, you have let the load fall from your shoulders, and a big healing surge will result from this release.

Begin your daily quiet times because you have been missing these on a deeper level than you realise, so make a special time each day for meditation. This quiet time serves everyone well, but the time has come to do more work with our book dictation. To begin with, the work will begin at odd times, but it will continue. The beloved Mary will assist in these endeavours because she has not finished her series yet. Her latest book was a stumbling block, but that is also an obstacle that has been overcome. Be aware of today's message because it comes with a bang.

*At this point, I bent to pick up something from the floor, and as I straightened up, I promptly banged my head hard on the table. Ouch! That is what I call an instant prediction.*

The essence of all heavenly messages is this: Open up to the Creator and immerse yourself in a subliminal connection to everything because each message will have extra knowledge as the end result, and that is emphatically that! All native and cultural stories, myths, legends, and holy writings are full of messages that have been offered for mankind's benefit.

Some images have become well known, such as floods, fires, burning bushes, plagues, and so on, but the interpretations in modern times have often been misused, misunderstood, altered beyond recognition, deleted, or forgotten. To be clear, let me say that the meanings in the messages are similar today as they were in the timeline before the biblical stories emerged.

The context and content of each spiritual message or sign needs to be understood clearly not only in the heart of each individual but also to all others belonging to a cultural or social group. These singular and multiple aspects cannot be separated. Indeed, how can you separate anything in your existence? One atom affects all atoms because all are joined to create the building blocks of life.

The given messages will not only be for personal enlightenment but will have importance for everyone and everything, and they will also have an integral part to play in the guidance and teaching of all who will listen. These messages, whatever the content, are beacons for you...the beacons that leads you Home.

*Samuel wrapped these words in a cushion of seriousness because this was an important sentence and it meant a lot to him that we understand what he was saying. And an odd thing to mention here, as he was saying the last sentence, an immense and deeply emotional surge swept through me; it was so strong it almost took my breath away. I felt the words resonate strongly.*

As a modern-day example of dual messages, let me explain this event. Early this morning, a meteor shower lit up the starry night sky. Some people watched this heavenly display with curiosity, some with scientific detachment, some disinterested, and others awed. But some people will have understood this magnificent display in a more intuitive and comprehensive manner.

This beautiful shower of starlight and power was a fiery display celebrating the opening of mankind's heart chakra because it was a physical display celebrating the understanding of the basic connection between all Universal Energy. This was a flowering and releasing of godly energy that will connect with all people who were aware and receptive to this powerful vibration.

Did you take into your matrix some of this magical power? Did you open your heart and acknowledge the bigger picture that was being shown to you at this time? You didn't have to know the questions that this display answered; all you had to do was open up to the Creator's wisdom and both the question and answers would have been known by you.

Primitive cultures have always watched the heaven for signs and portents, and even if the message was off centre when it was deciphered, it would have been seen as a sign or message from their Creator of choice, and they would have reacted to this message accordingly. They understood they were a part of the Heavens, not isolated and apart, because successful cultural survival depended on this important connection.

Today, much of this awe and connectedness has been forgotten. In the current day and age, the scientific aspect tends to smother the spiritual side of these heavenly events. This dichotomy will vanish, but not today and not tomorrow.

Let me tell you this, many Workers of the Light are bringing back into the public's awareness the bigger Spiritual picture, and understanding of the link between Universal bits and pieces and each Soul's inner core. There is a deep rumbling of understanding going on and getting stronger, and this connection is broiling under the surface of people's consciousness. It is cleaning away the dross.

Coming soon to a place near you, there will be an eruption of reawakened memory! The blindfolds will be thrown aside, the heart core will blossom with the connection of all Souls, and the language will change to one of all-knowing. You, and you, and you will know who you are, from whence you came, and why you are on Earth's surface in a physical body at this time. You will know and understand the Music of the Spheres, the Dance of Light, and the Singing of the Angels. You will remember you.

Now, the timing of these heavenly activities is important. The selected example of the meteor shower in this timeline is important. All who understand symbology in any way will see that this event was not just a small shower of meteor particles burning up in Earth's atmosphere; they will see the significance in the light patterns. It was God's visible umbrella being spread for all mankind to see.

*There was such a wonderful feeling of fun, good spirits and humour about, with big smiles and happiness aplenty. The meteor shower spread across the sky, and it spread from a focal point and spread out in a sparkling fan shape. The umbrella description is quite apt and I was mesmerised, awed and very emotional by the sheer size of the spectacle.*

This suggests that protection of a major kind is being offered to mankind. And this offered help and protection was, and is, still there for everyone who accepts it, thus enabling them to survive the coming turbulent times. This sign was overt; it was out there in the open for all to see, because it was not hidden away in a dusty tome, carefully locked away in some secret and forbidden library. It was freely and universally offered.

This example of the meteor is just one of many I could have chosen to talk about. I give this as an example because of the timing of the event. Many layers of meaning can be picked up by the questioning people who bother to connect with these wonderful events. Is this a message from the Creator? Or is it a message from another planetary source?

Why does this look like a protective umbrella? Is it a dire warning for mankind, a warning to prepare for adverse conditions? Is it a signpost pointing mankind towards safety?

All of the above is true, and more besides. Did you really think the meteor shower was a geographical, clinical, and unemotional event you just happened to witness? Or did you actually feel an unfamiliar tug at your heart strings, coupled with a strange feeling that you didn't quite understand?

Many such events will come swiftly and surely into the Universe around you, because the vibrational intensity is rising in your personal and universal spaces. You are being given the chance to leap joyfully into a new level of existence, with your hand being held by the Angels of Creation as you are led safely through the tumultuous times. Do you choose or not choose to take this helping hand as you move into a new dimension? It's your choice.

The signs and events of the New Age for mankind are quite obvious to most people and will need little interpretation. Some people will not see or want to see the obvious, so for them confusion and uncertainty will be an overriding response to any prophetic signs. And this will cloud any tiny bit of clear sightedness already there and make it harder for new thoughts to work through situations as they arise. If people are confused and dithering about, either unable or reluctant to makes choices, then they are certainly not doing themselves any favours and, indeed, they are doing no one else favours either. They may unwittingly be affecting their friends who are actually trying to follow through on their intuitive hunches.

Uncertainty and dithering are catching, and it is easy to sow seeds of doubt even in an aggressive and strongly held belief system. So, who are these ditherers who cannot make up their minds about what they see happening around them? Who are the ones who cannot work out why things happen as they do, and why the ensuing effects evolve as they do?

Now, September 11th 2001 will go down in history as an important date for students of the future to remember.

*On this day, multiple airborne terrorist attacks flattened the Twin Trade Centre Towers in New York City, USA, and also damaged the Pentagon. It was an effective terrorist attack on the trade*

*and military centres of America. Both towers of the Trade Cen-*
*tre completely collapsed, with the loss of almost 3,000 lives. These*
*actions triggered a massive retaliation against terrorists based in*
*Afghanistan.*

But in what context will these students of the future
remember these actions? As a symbolic gesture to bring global
attention to the greed and power of the world's financial mar-
kets? Or as the day that westernised populations were made
aware that aggressive actions in foreign lands, instigated for
whatever the reason, can and may be returned in kind?

I suggest it will be neither of the above. The incident will
be recorded as a crime against the American people, and it will
be skewed until only a specific and dogmatic aspect is left to
live in the history books. The blinkers will be pulled down over
the eyes of the uncaring and non-curious.

The bombings in New York on that September 11th were
devastating, and these significant events were not recorded in
a fully and truthful 'big picture' way. It is up to the powers that
be, especially the ones who control the media, to bring a wider
and truer perspective to this tragic time. The underlying issues
needed to be brought out of the closet and it's only by offering
this full disclosure that the general populace will get a more
truthful picture of what is going on and what is being done in
their name.

Do you see any sign that the population demanded this
extra hidden information from their leaders? So far, there have
been few pertinent questions asked by Western citizens in general, and this behaviour follows established human behavioural
patterns that have flowed from previous historical experiences.

*These are interesting comments. Of course, there have been*
*many words written on these monumental events, but Samuel*

*seemed to be sliding beneath the daily news outlets, the in-depth analysis, and the blame game to talk about the underlying 'big picture' reasons and how the questions need to have intuitive leanings. He was getting into the personal emotional responses and the moral fibre and strength of character needed to work out the how and why these events happened on our 'watch'.*

It is a human foible to feel safer inside your comfort zone, and you also know if you stand above the crowd and draw attention to yourself, it can mean your head is in danger of being lopped off. And this symbolic beheading, like the tall poppy syndrome in action, may not be triggered by any action you actually make, but because you have stepped out of anonymity and made others feel uncomfortable and guilty; and for this, you will be targeted.

This is not an idle statement. To see someone doing what you lack the moral fibre to do brings forth anger, discomfort, guilt, and heartache about your own lack of faith and courage. It brings fear out into the open, where you personally have to deal with it.

When a big event such as the September 11th event is in the news, it confronts everyone in their home on a daily basis. So, do you avidly watch the newscasts and exalt in the chase for the baddies, but when the media is turned off, you forget about it all? Or do you pause for a moment and try to work out what is really going on, and if the timing is somehow important to you?

This upsetting scenario is being repeated time and time again in your living room, so do you in your personal spaces feel emotional trauma because of the bombing devastation that comes from tactical decisions or miscalculations by armed aggressors from either side of any conflict? Or maybe you do not react at all, and do not bother to ask any questions because you think it has nothing to do with you?

Let me tell you truly, if this is so, then you blank out these images and questions at your own peril. Every person is intrinsically connected to each bomb that is dropped, and with each stream of rhetoric that is spewed from the mouths of aggressors. You are a part of it all whether you live in an igloo in the Arctic or a stone hut in the Andes. There is no section on the planet that is not, in a major way, deeply connected to this major sign of change being played out on the World's stage.

The wealthy man on his yacht, the poor coal miner working deep within the earth, and the hungry child on the streets of a bustling city are all connected and in their individual way are influencing what publicity is seen by the global citizens.

Will the news be shown as blaring newscasts that condemn the 'baddies', or will there be a thorough discussion that covers all aspects of the action? Will the reasons for the actions be openly slammed by strident media, or the reasons shown as universal messages that can be deciphered in a new and comprehensive manner?

I am using the New York bombings as one example of a major sign for mankind, and one that needs to be understood in a big picture way. Many similar events and situations are happening around the world and each event, whatever type it is, needs to be seen as an open book of information. Most so-called tragic events will trigger similar reactions from the world populations. But I ask this: the event is tragic for whom?

This is a controversial question because I say it is certainly not tragic for the dead and dying. They have used their courage to choose to experience the next step of their existence. Maybe they are momentarily afraid, but the inner choice or decision to change was accepted and acted upon.

Tragic for the ones left behind? Again, confronting only momentarily, and even if you feel you are the victim of a tragedy, this is the time to be a creative person and sift through the rubble of whatever potentiality is there. Tragic events also bring into the light the magnificent qualities of the human spirit, and the enduring knowledge—or the opportunity to be reminded of the knowledge—that the Soul truly lives on. It is an eternal, infinite Spark of God.

This is the major thing that needs to be remembered while in the physical state. Therefore, think of this, the victims of tragic events are not only allowing themselves a chance to remember who they really are, but they are giving others around them who are connected with the events a chance to throw off their blindfolds and blinkers and let free their own inner memories. What a compassionate and brave thing to do!

So... victims? No, there are never victims in any time, place, or situation. There are only Souls who have, in a pre-planned way, chosen to go through a learning experience that will bring enlightenment to themselves as well as to others. Do you feel the people who died in the September bombings died for no reason? Do you think it was all a nasty accident, and that all the people who died were totally ignorant of their coming death? Or as I would prefer to say, their next experience?

Each and every person who was connected in any way knew what was to happen, and on a soul level agreed to participate in the action. This statement applies to all involved, not just the dead, the injured, the witnesses, and the volunteers, but to the helpers of all ilks, and the vast numbers of media viewers.

Everyone knew on some level what was to happen and, in a collective way, agreed to participate as a gesture of strength and physical manifestation so that troublesome questions would be brought out into the open. Like a helpful genie who takes the lid off the box that no one really wants to look into, maybe they knew what was inside but didn't want to deal with it.

Liken the New York bombings to the lid being blown off the box that contains unpalatable truths for both mankind's and Mother Earth's survival. The lid was literally smashed off.

What now? How do you deal with all these truths that have now been freed and taken wing? Do you get out your gun and shoot them down? There is nothing you can do that will put these truths, and these multiple questions, back in the box. This is the nature of signs and symbolic messages. They cannot be made to disappear, and even when ignored, they will repeat and repeat themselves until a positive action or awareness of them has been activated.

Do you shoot the messenger? Many people in many cultures have tried this during mankind's interesting history, but it does not stop the message from being remembered. Once said, words are non-returnable. You cannot put the towers in New York City back again. The message has already been given and is out in the open for all to see.

Have you listened only to the words and rhetoric of the political or social leaders, or have you used your own brain cells and delved through your own thoughts on these tragic events? When you see such major signs as these happening, do you know what questions to ask? Do you see this as a global event that encompasses much more than just isolated acts of terrorism?

Have you pondered about Mother Earth's reaction to the heavy bombardment and heavy damage on a mountain range, in a country far from where you live? Do you wonder if this pounding has damaged energy grids that, when intact, help stabilise the world as you know it? Have you had thoughts about why terrorism exists in the first place? Have you thought at any time that you don't really know what questions to ask and where to go for answers?

Even if you haven't bothered to think things through, you still must realise you are a multi-talented person with inner power and strength, and with unlimited intuitive knowledge, so how can you not be bothered to investigate any unpalatable truths that have flown out of the box?

As a part of the collective human consciousness, you are an accessory in some minor or major way, to all acts of unpleasantness, be it terrorism in some form, tragic events in some form, and whether they are either local or global events. All events that play out on the world stage are the build-up, and then the physical release of this collective human consciousness.

Of course, there is the other aspect, the other side of the proverbial coin, the collective consciousness of universal love, light, and beautiful experiences. These also have their physical manifestation, but in lovely events and happenings, and with these you also are an accessory in either a minor or major way.

It is a balancing act that is continually going on, and everyone's inner thoughts, unexpressed emotions, desires, and intents freely shift this balance point between 'negative' and 'positive' outcomes. It is all a part of learning and enlightenment, the see-sawing, the walking the path of love, or stumbling over another path when blinkers are in place. These blinkers may be worn deliberately or worn because of ignorance and laziness.

Mankind is teetering on a breakthrough of a major understanding. This Age has been predicted since the beginning of
the timeline as you know it to be. A major transformation of
the species is imminent, and the signposts, the global events of
importance, the turbulence, and the actions and reactions will
increase in intensity and frequency as inner transformation and
true remembering strengthens. The troubled times will continue yet, because when dramatic lessons are being constantly
enacted it is an extremely effective classroom.

Wake up, mankind. I use the term mankind—it may not
always be politically correct, but I have always used it. The time
comes when the see-saw tips to one side and does not rise
again. Do you want to be on the end that is going nowhere, or
do you want to be on the end that opens the way for expan-
sion and new beginnings? Do you feel confident you will go to
Heaven and sit on a cloud with God?

Do you understand, or even care to understand, the lessons that humanity is giving itself now? If you do care, then
read on. If you don't care, coming soon to a bus stop near you
is a bus that you will never have the chance to catch...even if
you change your mind at the last moment and want to climb
onboard. Sorry, but the bus will go swishing by without you.

# 2

# ON BEING A GOOD PERSON

Have you made a start by aligning yourself to the winning or more enlightened side of events? Have you truly begun to do this? Have you started going back to your church or place of worship on a regular basis, and being a good person who sits quietly on a pew each service, listening to and agreeing with the sermons offered, then singing or responding only when asked to?

Of course, being this good and obedient person will get your name ticked off in the attendance book. But what else do you do?

Do you do anything else to make you feel good about being obedient to the rules and regulations of the service? Do you put any personal energy into the devotions, and into the communal prayers you join in with? Do you personally expend emotional energy with heartfelt and unconditional love, joy, thankfulness, and godly love as you say the words of service? Or do you sit like a good-mannered lump and watch the clock ticking slowly towards 'get out of church time'?

Despite how these questions read, I am not anti-church or against any religious belief system that has a ritualistic programming. I am totally against the domineering rules and regulations that seem to have taken over the common sense of the people who created the rituals and rites in the first place, despite the good, bad, or indifferent reasons used at the time. If you blindly follow each rule without question, it is you who loses your personal power to others; in fact, you give it away.

This may sound presumptuous of me to say this, so please hear me out. As an example, let us say, you are required to kneel at a certain time during a service. It doesn't matter what kind of service; any kind will do to illustrate this point. So, you kneel at the indicated time, with everyone else. You keep in time and in synchronicity with them, so that you do not stand out from the crowd.

Do you know why you kneel at the specific times that you are asked to do so? Do you ever wonder why this needs to happen at these specific times? Is it to bring a sense of community and fellowship into the worship? Is it to break the service into bite-sized, digestible pieces? Or is this action included for some other reason?

I assume you have at least pondered on these questions. To be a regular attendee in a group situation and not to have thought about these actions you are asked to do is simply incomprehensible to me. The issue of organised ritual is an emotional one, and to have a meaningful and emotional output implies that you have at least found out when and why you are emoting at specific times.

*There was a strong, dry sense of humour flickering about the desk as these words were being recorded. I got the impression that Samuel has seen a lot of strange ceremonies, rigid rituals, and everything else in between, in his long association with the devout peoples of the Ages. Devout or dutiful seems to be the question he was interested in at this moment.*

So, maybe you love your God and become emotional when you pray to Him. At this time, a note to clarify a point: God is a 'He', sometimes a 'She', or sometimes everything in-between, in this book. The words are totally interchangeable if you are into gender naming. I am very aware that the Creator God is an Everything—and, in fact, is more than the sum of everything, but I do need to put something down, so will go with the flow so to speak.

There is no disrespect intended, and I will assume many will feel God is of masculine gender, because this is what has been commonly taught before and during your times. This fact may be neither right nor wrong, and it is not the issue here. That is for another time to be talked about. This 'loving' emotion you may feel in church or in a place of worship feels good, doesn't it? The minister, the priest, the pastor, and even your own feelings tell you it is a 'feel good' situation. My question is "Good for what?"

Don't get angry, dear pious reader, this is a valid question and I am extremely interested in your answers. May I even suggest a few possible ideas?

1. Good for your soul.
2. Makes you feel good, as though you are doing something worthwhile.
3. It is what you are told to believe, and what you read in various texts: that you have to love God.
4. Everyone else says they do it, and you want to do the same.

5. You truly believe you open up to Spirit/God; a heart connection is there.

6. The religious tomes tell you to love the Creator; you are an obedient person, so you do.

7. Lady friends will like you better, if they see that you love God. Or if you are female, then male friends will like you more.

8. It gives you peace, and good feelings.

These are just a few answers to 'good for what' that pop into my thoughts at this time. Have you already thought of any of these answers? Because there is a mountain of answers to choose from. However, you will miss the point of this whole exercise if you don't look for clarity about the 'good for what' question firstly within your intuitive self where all answers reside.

Now, here is another question to ponder over. How do you know if you love a God in the right way? All the Scriptures give surprisingly scrambled messages about the Supreme Being, and over the many civilizations, the interpretation of these messages leaves a great deal of truth lying out in the dust of antiquity.

You walk through a mine field in trying to work out your religious affiliations, don't you? It is not always easy to be good, when each time you listen to religious teachings, new interpretations may be put into familiar wordage, and even these new interpretations may seem reasonable at the time, despite coming from a different angle than the one you are comfortable with.

To truly love God/The Creator/Great Spirit/Allah/All There Is/the Supreme One, or whatever name you choose, is to bypass constitutional teachings and go straight to the Source. Even going to the Source may give you scrambled messages at first, because you could have unintentionally blinkered yourself into a learning rut. And if that is so, it becomes difficult to see and sense new ideas and intuit new insights. However, by going straight to the Source, you have many great spiritual Teachers waiting in the Realm of Spirit ready to step into the classroom, and gently steer you onto the correct path called 'understanding.'

Of course, you can be a conscientious churchgoer and prac- tise heart to heart loving with your God, but it is not always easy to keep intentions pure and the concentration focused. It is not easy to put aside generations of conditional learning. After all, you may feel if it was good enough for your great grand- parents, grandparents, or parents, it is indeed good enough for you. Right? Wrong. You are not your ancestors, and you are not your parents; all that your ancestral family has done is helped steer you towards familiar circumstances and given you a base to begin from. As a unique individual, you are meant to walk your own path in all ways, especially spiritual ways.

Church and structured rituals may give you a comfort- able zone in which to balance yourself, so that you can then take that next step into the Light of Knowledge. You see, you are not meant to be just good, you are meant to be godly. That shocks you? It shouldn't, because as you know in your heart of hearts, the Creator doesn't sit on a big fleecy white cloud up in Heaven. The Creator Energy is within you, and this energy is one and the same as your spark of life. You are godly from the time of the Beginning, and it is now time for mankind to remember this fact. And to remember the power, the consequences, and the reason that this is the Time of the Homecoming.

So, to my way of seeing things, a good churchgoer may be performing all the correct responses at all the correct times, but I am more interested in the personal level of understanding of the Creator Within. This Inner God is the one you pray to, sing to, and meditate to. You knew that, didn't you? Every Great Teacher who has ever walked the Earth has taught this lesson clearly and well. Have you learnt this lesson? Or have you learnt it and then conveniently forgotten it? Many people do forget this, because to believe and to understand it fully brings all responsibility fairly and squarely onto your shoulders... responsibility for everything that is created around you, to you, for you, and in the past, present, and future.

If you say no, that it is not so, then you show to all that you are afraid to believe in the God Within, in the godliness of you. And if this is so, it is such a shame because you are quite a nice person. And despite hiding under an inner blanket of fear and disbelief that is maybe out of sight and out of mind most of the time, you do have your Inner God working full time on your behalf. This God Within does not take holidays, does not take sick leave, and does not advise anything that is not in your best interest.

What a shame if you hide away this special part of yourself and feel too scared to allow it come out into the Light. So, sing your praises, say your prayers, bow your head, and kneel when it is time to do so, but please, please do these actions with the knowledge of the Creative Spark Within. This connection will make you an effective and enlightened powerhouse person.

For the non-churchgoer, the same words apply. You do not need a building to pray in or to talk to your Creator in. This communication can be done anywhere, anytime, awake, asleep, or even up a tree, and maybe while swimming in the lake. Each individual is different [thank the Creator Within] and all the pathways meander towards the Inner Energy gestalt, and all in the most amazing of ways.

You can show the love of the God within by connecting honestly with a pebble from the riverbed, or with a leaf from the tree in front of your house. Many religions have known that the Inner God encompasses you, all floras and fauna, minerals, and everything in between. The shamanic cultures have known and practised the connection to the Love of All things. Of course, this is a generalisation because some have a fear-based belief, but the principle of personal inter-connections is there.

Therefore, some people may find a comfortable base from which to begin understanding their God within a building, and some people will find they are more connected and inspired by the majesty of the natural worlds. It doesn't matter as long as each and every one becomes aware that *they* are individually and collectively responsible for their spiritual progress—not a minister of religion, priest, shaman, or the psychic lady next door. One cannot escape or give away this responsibility. It is there for you to deal with it.

Okay, you may argue, what about the person who doesn't believe in God, a person who is nasty, who hurts people, or one who kills bugs with glee? What about them? Why aren't they forced in some way to be more responsible for themselves and the results of their actions? Why isn't their 'God Within' trying to do something to stop the pain and suffering they are causing to others? What about it?

*It was now four days since the last book dictation. There had been some lovely rain, and everything was clean and crisp outside.*

*At any given time, it is always my decision whether to receive or go ahead and record the book dictation. The option is always there to do this recording, but sometimes other things get in the way.*

*At this point in time, it felt as though a lot was happening around me in both the spiritual and physical sense, and I was in the middle of a huge puzzle that I needed to quickly work out. I tried to connect to the different vibrations that seem to swirl around me, I tried to work out what it is that I was meant to be doing or not doing, what signals were meant for me in a personal way, and how to read these correctly.*

*Maybe the lesson here was not to try. Even though no book recording was done for a few days, the contacts with my friends in spirit had not stopped.*

*I had just reread Samuel's original essay almost six years after it was written; the magical day when I attempted to begin doing legible automatic writing. I could still feel the high voltage energy, the sheer joy, and the feeling of celebration—the power that was in the room. It was a profound experience indeed.*

*Each time I begin to write Samuel's dictation, I try to 'go with the flow' a little more, instead of focusing on the vibrations that pique my curiosity or trying to work out what will be written or happen at the time of writing.*

*I was trying to dampen this curiosity, so that I had no preconceived thoughts about the subject matter that was being written about. With the Mary books I would have phrases, sentences, subjects, and insights coming fully formed into my mind, but even then, I was continually being surprised at the way the beloved Lady expressed her ideas.*

*Here, Samuel was bringing a different energy to the equation. It is hard to explain but the words seemed to slam into my brain and embed themselves deeply. It was a whole new ballgame, and I often had little idea of the paragraph meaning until it was read later. I thought, as this new work progresses, I would be in for an entertaining and challenging time. When dictation began again, it was as though there was no hiatus of any kind.*

The days of blindly following the normal rituals are coming to an end. Do you still feel relaxed and comforted after your routine Sunday church visit? That is very good, very good indeed if that is the case; but you need to know how to continue this feeling of 'goodness and peace to all men' in a more constant and empowering way.

What is the point in walking out of a place of worship and feeling great about all things, and even before you get home, you lose the peace plot and all your good intentions? Maybe another driver cut in front of you on the road, or little Johnny vomited on the back seat of the car? Living with the God within means living in a State of Grace, and this includes when little Johnny is being sick all over your Sunday best shoes. Can you say, dear readers, that this State of Grace is the way you are behaving and feeling at all times?

Do you feel at one with the Universe? Do you feel the energy ties and silver cords that connect you to everything and everyone around you? Can you honestly say that you are in this State of Grace as I write, and as you read what I have written? In truth, very few people will be, so do not go knocking your head against the wall if you feel you have failed this test.

*This was interesting, and I was getting to appreciate Samuel's wry sense of humour. The swirls of fun, laughter, and witticism were flooding the work area. And there was a lot of energy zapping around my head, so strong it was distracting.*

Well, don't let me stop you knocking your head against the wall; at least by doing this you will feel, in a physical manner, a connection to the world around you.

*The humour was palpable; there was a great sense of fun, silly images, and big guffaws of laughter shaking things up. I loved it!*

The State of Grace is your innate state of existence, and it is so difficult at times to remember that you don't need to chase anything to be able to find this peaceful and loving state. It is within you, always within you, so the only direction you need to look is inwards. The church, the meditation, the Earth Mother, and all helpers and teachers can assist you in this journey of discovery, but as you accept this help, I strongly suggest you be discerning.

Be aware at all times of what you are being told. Be aware of anyone with vested interests steering you away from the inner path or guiding your attention into a minefield of time-wasting activities. Be aware of what you are doing, and how you are reacting when amongst teachers of any ilk. And here I speak of both physical and spiritual teachers. You need to wake up and look after your own interests. Be discerning. Always take note of, and believe, your own inner intuitive responses.

As you listen to the teachings, ask these questions: Does this sermon have the ring of truth? Does the fear and damnation story feel true? Am I really guilty of something diabolical if I don't put $ 10 in the collection plate? Does the young boy sitting next to me know that he is going to Hell because he is chewing gum inside the church? Does all this sound logical?

And if the questions and the resulting answers do not feel right or sound logical and true to you, then why not? What nonsense has been said to make you consciously link the 'going to hell' belief with the chewing of gum in church?

Now, dear reader, you may think I have just written non-sense and if the truth be told, I have. So many of your foibles, worries, fears, panics, upsets, and so on have a very negative impact on all your emotions. It is absolutely nonsense if you are wasting and expending your God given energy on things that do not matter in the least.

The petty rules and regulations of society in general—whether they come from the east, west, south, north, in, out, up, or down, it doesn't matter in the slightest—fills the mind of mankind with thoughts that are busy and usually non-productive. This busyness can keep you from having the time and energy to go within and connect to your State of Grace. Maybe you have quiet moments when you are in this Godly zone but find it difficult to stay connected.

But do not be upset, because even the smallest amount of true connection will give you a wisdom boost, which will amplify this godly energy, which then strengthens and spreads this wisdom and grace into all other areas of your life. Quiet, stolen moments spent in the State of Grace will keep you going during your day-to-day experiences.

Again, I say that you don't need to sit in a religious circle to attain this connection. Each time your focus in the present is momentarily distracted or blurred, the inner 'you' is given a chance to come out of hiding and leave an impression or a piece of 'grace' in your consciousness. The trick is to allow the relaxation of this rigid control of focus, thus easing any blocks, freeing and allowing the access to your Inner God to flow smoothly.

As you walk around each day doing whatever you do to fill in the time, every now and then stop thinking of what is in front of your nose and tell yourself that you are now going to look deep inside and touch, feel, and sense your State of Grace. Try to do this as many times as you can remember during the day, and you will soon realise that it takes 'no time' at all. You can even do it while peeling the potatoes or driving the car.

*At this point, I asked the obvious question that may have popped into everyone's head after reading about this exercise. While driving the car? Or for safety reasons, doing any other activity that needs one to be done carefully? Is this safe to do?*

Alright, a point of clarification here, to have followed my words to this point you will have understood that what I speak of is not a dangerous activity.

*Samuel's humour was again making its presence felt. This time it was not a rib tickling guffaw but a gentle, persuasive and infectious chuckle, and I feel I need to find new ways of describing what I am feeling and sensing, because Samuel's words are always accompanied by different energy and emotions.*

Some of you may indeed wonder if this driving and defocusing is safe. Yes, indeed, this is safe. If you defocus your mental busyness about the driving and all that it entails, and fleetingly connect to the inner you, you can actually increase your driving awareness. You can bring in such a powerhouse of awareness you will be a better driver.

Defocusing does not mean stopping your brain function or sitting crossed legged on a shaggy mat on the floor, or even crossing your eyes in concentration in your effort to blank out everything around you. You don't have to meditate for a long time.

The instantaneous inner connections bypass the bumpy roadblocks of your life and immediately light up your life. You see more clearly, react faster and surer, become aware in a more powerful and safer way of how you are driving, and what terrain you are driving through, and so forth. You awaken your senses, not dampen them.

This quick exercise is a fleeting peek and connection to your Spark Plug, your generator, or whatever image you bring to mind of your Inner God or Intuitive Heart. If you do this exercise enough times, you wear a track or groove into this inner strength, so each flick of your awareness towards this focus goes along a more defined path. The journey becomes faster and easier. The flicking back and forth of your awareness brings a balance and inner strength to your daily 'in your face' situations around you. It could be a slow change at first, but the more you bring your conscious and unconscious energies together, the stronger the intuitive information flows.

Gradually, you will sense a change in how you perceive the world around you in your daily life. You will begin to see things going on about you with new eyes, and with new understanding. This flickering back and forward between the conscious and unconscious and intuitive mind levels becomes a new state of experience, a level of unifying energy that is yours to utilise. A new state of aliveness emerges and stays with you at all times. You carry your State of Grace with you in an aware and meaningful way at all times.

This is a powerful way to live your life. You use your State of Grace as a part of your existence; you live with this wonderful and powerful universal energy as a natural and integral part of your matrix. So, it is quite simple to bring the church or religious devotions into daily life so long as you leave behind the petty rules and regulations. Sweep the emotions clean of chaff, and go straight to the good grains of Truth and Love within.

It is imperative that each and every soul living at this time leaves the clutter of man-made religious rules to the side and walks the inner path of Truth—because this inner truth is the True Truth, the Divine Truth that harbours within it all knowledge of the Universe, of What Is, What Will Be, and What Needs to Be. Many teachers will tell you this truth. Many more teachers are still to come who will teach the same lessons. Truth is truth whether hidden under social garbage or shining above the rainbow. Truth is truth. It does not change.

*This was the end of chapter 2. It wasn't until a week or so later that the book dictation resumed. This delay was totally of my doing. At times there seems to be some reluctance on my part to jump fully into this experience, and this bothers me a lot because when the recording goes smoothly, and on a regular schedule, it is an extremely rewarding and uplifting experience.*

*In that moment, I was giving myself feelings of guilt over not recording the offered dictation. This was a weird situation. I knew all that was written has profound lessons for me as well, and I kept shuffling between trying to work out these lessons and trusting freely in the Universe.*

*Try or not try? Trust in the process of the words being written? I get the most wonderful sense of comfort and benevolence when the sessions are in progress and frequently, Samuel will comment on what I am feeling at the end of the daily session, or at the beginning of the next one. Sometimes weeks pass between the sessions, and my guilt increases.*

*I know I accepted the offer to work with the Spirits on recording the offered words of wisdom, but maybe I do get overwhelmed by how it is all panning out. It is a huge undertaking and as the mountains of words pile up, I wonder sometimes if I am up to the task. A comforting word is always welcomed, such as the following:*

Dearest daughter. Here is a personal word for you. Dearest daughter, please trust in yourself. Do not go looking for vague reasons for this or that. Just decide to jump off the proverbial cliff and fly. You know you can and will fly. Allow no other option to enter your thoughts and feelings.

As we do these sessions, we will help you to see why you have been fussing and faltering. Daily sessions are very effective because they set up a pattern and highlight energy pathways that become easier and easier to use.

You have been picking up on, and sensing, the state of these paths better than you realise. Some days the energy flow is not as clear as others. Each day, each moment, is a new day, a new moment, so please never forget this fact.

# 3

# AWAKENING THE TEACHERS

When we see the World in chaos, the Spiritual/God Helpers who reside in a different reality to you do what is possible by working as a collective force to restore harmony across all levels. We are able to help in many ways. You may hear this question time and time again:

"How can a spirit, or whatever these people or personalities really are, help us down here on Earth? If they have no bodies, how can they help us?"

Have you ever heard someone say this? I am willing to wager a rainbow that you have heard this question at one time or another, or at least one very similar. It is a tired old saying or comment that is brought out into the open each time someone's ignorance is trying to be hidden from others.

What is implied here is a total lack of understanding on how a human is created and formed, how a human life is lived and then 'dies'. There is a lack of understanding of even the basics of Universal Law.

Firstly, we who reside in other levels of reality are not 'people'. We cannot be labelled like this, because there are many layers of interweaving realities within each energy level, with each level being the home base for whomever, or whatever, is more compatible and at ease in the particular vibrational environment. All creation is moving, like dancing motes of pure energy, and these motes all dance to different rhythms.

Can you imagine a Universe that is like a cosmic onion with layers and layers all dancing and vibrating at different speeds, but at the same time, all interacting with each other and all in unison to make a Whole? Try to imagine this huge Cosmic onion as layers, yet the onion aroma interpenetrates and permeates everywhere. The levels make one Cosmos, not many separate ones. Of course, differences do occur, but all meld together beautifully.

You need to understand that what you see about you with your wonderful eyes and feel with your fingers is just one tiny level or layer of vibrational energy, and these vibrations dance to a similar and familiar rhythm. It is this layer of your physical world of manifestation that your Inner God is learning to experience, experiment with, and create with, because most other levels are just out of focus for the moment.

This is how the schoolroom has been arranged. Imagine the teacher tapping the blackboard with a pointer; all eyes in the classroom are meant to see the specific area that the pointer is indicating. The focus is on this spot, yet the rest of the classroom doesn't disappear, does it? It is all there, the desks, windows, slates, books, pencils, charcoal, and so on—all still there.

If you are learning your lessons by following guidelines, you concentrate on the point of interest and do not notice your surroundings. They have not disappeared into nothingness. You see, you have this amazing God-given ability to know things. You know the desk and chairs are still there because your energy matrix is a part of, and is intrinsically connected with, these objects. Your energy does not stop at your skin or at the edge of your energy bubble.

You are a multi-knowing, multi-talented person, and your blueprint has been implanted with a connection to everything. I will repeat this... Everything. It is what you concentrate on at any given time that becomes the most immediate presence, but you still have a total connection to everything else.

The same applies to us, those who live in other vibrational levels. Unless you bother to focus on our level, you will not see or sense us, and because you don't see or sense us, you may begin to doubt that we do indeed exist. You forget you know about us, and indeed are actually a part of us and our worlds.

Are you following what I am saying here? The person who says we cannot help with the physical issues you are dealing with has forgotten his or her divine strengths and connections. And that is a shame because on the intuitive level, this person is in constant contact with us and the God Spark within. And because of this connection, what is done in one area or level will always ripple out and affect all other realities.

There is no such thing as a place/event/result/action or reaction that does not affect all other layers of vibrational realities. Of course, the biggest ripple or action will be in the immediate area where the action was initiated, such as when a stone is dropped into a pond, and here the strongest ripples are at the point of activation. The ripples created flow from this point across the water, but they do not stop at the water's edge. They ripple out over the land, below the earth, and up into the air. These waves will change in intensity and type, but the movement is never stopped.

Do you see what I am trying to say in simple words and everyday imagery? We, from the Spirit Worlds, impact, impinge, and permeate on all other worlds or levels of existence: your physical level is only one such level. We are all connected by divine energy. It stands to reason that we can help in so many ways. All you need to do is to read the Holy Books of each civilization and see in words, both ancient and new, the many references to the Spiritual Worlds reacting and interweaving with the physical world.

This has been happening since time began, so to say to your friends that you do not believe this interaction occurs, and that it cannot happen, shows to others that you are a sad and lonely person who has shut down even your logical thinking processes. It shows someone who has lost their way and cannot see the Light because of the shadows, and who cannot connect with the Divine impulses that would help remove these shadows and let the Light radiate freely into their personal world.

Unfortunately, this is now a common enough situation in the modern world. Too many souls have lost their inner knowing, their inner understanding of the magical energy strands that make up the Universe they are part of. It is like living in the dancing colours of a rainbow yet being unable to see these colours. What sadness! What desolation of the soul this lack brings! The hope is lost and the Light dims. This is not a happy situation for any Child of God.

*At this point, Samuel ended the session although I felt that I could keep going for a while yet. I had just idly wondered if my plants on the back porch were getting enough sun, whether the morning sun was enough for good health. Then I realised that Samuel had been writing about bringing in more light.*

*When the words come, they can come to me already fully formed in my head, not usually as a 'voice'; they seem to be just there. If my focus wanders from the rolling script... and it sometimes does... I lose the continuity of what is being said unless the intensity of the incoming words is strong and pushy.*

*Yet now and again these outside thoughts pop in, like those about the plants on the porch. When this happens, I feel I am goofing off and become annoyed or cross with myself. But later, as I reread what has been written, these impulsive thoughts bring an everyday analogy to my attention that explains simply the aspects being written about. So, there is this juggling of my focus during these book dictation sessions, and I am learning to trust the wayward thoughts that come drifting into my head.*

*They seem to be a part of the whole process. Of course, the plants on the porch will be sad if they don't get enough sunlight, the same as us. If we don't allow enough light into our lives, we will feel the lack. We can watch the plants, and if they do not thrive, move them into a new position where they can get more light on their leaves.*

*But what do we do when we see people who are not thriving because of a lack of the Light within? Move them into a new position? What if they are so used to the spot they are in, they do not want to be moved? Or are afraid to move? What if their 'roots' are deeply and securely imbedded into the soil at the place they choose? Do we cut through the roots? Do we traumatise them for their own good?*

*Interesting situations can develop from this line of thought, because who is to judge whether someone needs more light? Not me, because I have trouble looking after me! It is only each individual who can choose to stay or to move. Maybe there are lessons being learned in the darker places where they are, or maybe there has been a temporary forgetting that there is Light just around the corner. It's a dance, isn't it? It is another level of dance, and each step brings change of one sort or another.*

Even as Spirits or Spirit Personalities, we are able to help in the physical aspects of mankind in more ways than you in your present state may remember. This help ranges from sending love into loveless situations, to physically manifesting into your vibrational dimension and bringing a more immediate presence into any given scenario. Everyone who has an opinion to express will tell you to believe what you see with your own eyes, whether those eyes are in good working order or not.

Now, we cannot just do what we would want or wish to do; there are some rules and Cosmic regulations that even we need to follow. We need to be always aware that the help, advice, and the teachings are all geared to the specific path that encourages your enlightenment and empowerment in all ways. By doing this, we help you find the Path to Home.

There are so many, many paths, and so many ways to walk each one. In our own funny, quirky, diabolical, effective, and unusual way we can assist you in these life journeys by pointing out options you may not always see before your nose, and these options will be brought to your attention in a myriad of ways.

This may be through hearing a friend talking about something you need to know about at the time, an inner hunch sneaking through your dogmatic belief barriers and shouting 'in your face' before it can be waved aside, a butterfly landing on your nose just as you ask for confirmation about something, being drawn to a certain colour while you are trying to work out a problem, being invited outside by someone and given the chance to interact with the Natural Kingdoms, dreaming options, and scenarios unlimited.

We can be subtle, we can be direct, and the help and advice so given will always empower, enlighten, and enrich you, even if you do not think so at the time.

Never will our input lead you away from Home. The old saying 'For your highest good' reigns supreme here, and this intention is always followed strictly, because as I have already mentioned, cosmic rules and regulations do not live exclusively in the physical worlds; they are the blueprint of all existence and need to be adhered to for the benefit of all Universal denizens.

In different levels, the rules are adapted to suit the locale, but the Prime Order stays the same. Therefore the 'Guides', 'Guardian Angels', 'Guardians', and 'Spirit Helpers' who are with you on your journey know these cosmic rules and will apply them at all times, because they know the cosmic rules also apply to themselves. Keep your heart open to receive this help, and know it is given lovingly, and that there is indeed a destination to focus upon. Open your heart and you will have allowed yourself to become aligned with a magnificent and practical team of Helpers.

Now, always, there is the other side of the coin. You can deliberately choose to align yourself with Helpers who do not always follow the cosmic rules and regulations to the degree expected. These are the Chaos Ones, and they will willingly go along with what you ask of them. When you ask the Chaos Ones to help you, you knowingly and consciously override your intuitive impulses and shut down your inner hunches. Your intuitive morality watchdog will become less effective, and it will struggle to remain in homeostasis.

Even without this balance, the morality factor will not stop working for your soul's personal benefit as best it can, despite how far you turn away from the inner light. You need to remember the bigger picture here, because in a persuasive way, and in a situation such as this, even the Chaos Ones are doing their cosmic job. They can help a person plumb the depths of emotion and despair, including all manner of experiences that are not generally considered to be happy ones.

Learning is done by living through a wide range of events that include the downs as well as the ups, as well as from the knowledge taught by the Great Teachers. What route to live by is a choice that is to be made by you alone; you follow the Inner God's signposts or turn from this and follow the longer detour.

You know, the final destination is always the same, so it does not matter what you do to get yourself lost in these detours; you will never have another destination to aim for. There is only one destination available.

Maybe you are feeling petulant or rebellious. By all means, take a detour, see, experience, and learn whatever you can, but even detours have an end, and petulant children outgrow their sulks and smile once again.

*Despite the harshness and bluntness of the words above, Samuel was wrapping them in good humour.*

*Now this is curious. In this later edit, while I am trying to come up with another way of saying how the subject is serious, yet Samuel was dictating it with humour, I made a typo and instead of typing 'good' as I intended, I typed in 'goose'. I think Samuel just made a valid point here.*

Once a rebel always a rebel is a saying that I am sure you all have heard in one language or another. Sorry, but that statement or belief isn't quite true. Nothing remains static. Nothing. Whether you see them or not, you have continual choices in front of you at all times, and by this continual choosing, a sliver of light can slip in between the rebellious moods and in some way, alter the paradigm of choice.

You see, the Good Guys and Gals never give up on a person who walks the detour called Chaos. Indeed, some of these souls have walked the hard and socially unacceptable path of trouble; and when at last, the glimmer of light eventually becomes focused upon, they can become strong advocates for teaching the Truth to others. Because of their own experiences, they are able to comprehensively and effectively explain the lessons that can be learnt in the Chaos and Anti Chaos detours. They have the personal experiences and examples to use as teaching aids, and they understand that what helped them may also help others.

So, good Angels, bad Angels: who cares? It all works well together as a whole schoolroom for you to learn and experience creativity in. We are the 'invisible' helpers, teachers, and friends, and the nemesis that will always help you align with the God Within. We can be sneaky or direct, and whatever it is you need to understand, you have unlimited help to do so. Don't forget this. Indeed, we can be called 'sneaky teachers' in many ways, or for very valid reasons. In day-to-day life, you may rarely notice our touch, guidance, or quiet whisper in your ear. It is only when your focus is turned towards us, to the God Within, that you remember the power of this larger dimension that is a part of you and you are always intrinsically connected with.

It is all quite fun and not to be taken as deadly serious. This might seem to be an inane statement at this point, because you may be one of the good citizens that know without doubt that hell and damnation is just around the corner if you don't continue to do the good things you have been taught to do, and if you do not follow all the rules of this and that. Right?

Wrong!

Creation is a Dance of Light, and a dance is a joyful, rhythmic movement. Let go of all the worries you have for an hour, get out into a place that is private and quiet, and just dance. You dance to your own tune, your own beat, so just open up your hands and let the light motes dance over them. Close your eyes and block out the wallpaper or the faded curtains. Make up your own scenery and dance within it. Smile, laugh, and tap your feet into the Earth's magical energy.

When you have danced, look about you. You will see that everything is still there—chairs, rug, and faded curtains—but you will find that it all seems more energised. You have given yourself a sparkle. You see and feel with an uplifted and different attitude.

You will have truly broken the hypnotic focus that was weighing heavily on your shoulders before the dance. Without trying, you have changed the way you react to life, and it was as simple as a dance, which may or may not have been graceful and coordinated.

Try and do this dance as often as you need to. Do this dance in private if you feel the need to move, and not in front of the many, because by doing it in front of an audience you may be dancing for the benefit of others and not for you personally. In front of other people, you may be feeling restricted, embarrassed, clumsy, or shy. Or you may feel exactly the opposite, because you may be a natural born exhibitionist and need to put on a good show for other people's benefit.

I speak here of a personal and private communion with the Creative Energy. So, you now have done your dance, and during this you found that you were not able to breathe very well. I tell you truly, don't be afraid of the breath of life; even it has its rhythms, and it may take several dances for you to get the feel of these rhythms again.

*The above chapter was dictated as the words spiralled onto the paper with glee. Even the pen wanted to circle and twirl, and to be honest I wanted to get up from the desk and have a twirl and spin myself. The words danced themselves onto the page! The whole room seemed to be in on the dance as well, and it was such fun to record. It is a strange but at the same time uplifting thing to experience.*

As you dance, feel us dancing with you. If you cannot actually feel or imagine this joyful movement personally, then imagine a group of people dancing, all swaying and moving to the beat, with light glittering from the robes and images around you. Enjoy this interlude and use it as a meditation process because it can be used as a time for letting down barriers and allowing Spirit to bring to you whatever love, help, teaching, and uplifting energy is needed at the time.

The Samuel in the biblical stories is portrayed as a stern, unbending man—a man of influence and judgement. Well, do not believe all aspects written about every character, because much has been altered, lost, and forgotten. In my biblical days I loved music, so can you find that piece of information written anywhere in the books?

And this musical love has been a continuing source of comfort, love, and enjoyment to me down through the Ages. Music is a cosmic vibration and symbol, and the more you connect with this heartbeat, the clearer the paths become between realities. The clearer the pathway, the clearer the communication between vibrational levels.

It stands to reason that if you are holding yourself rigidly in a good citizen posture and mode, I give you permission to relax and enjoy life a little more. Life is a dance of creativity, and it needs to be expressed in a joyous and gleeful way. The weight of the world is not on your shoulders, you only think it is, so allow us to help you remove this burden of thought and heaviness from you.

Authorise the God Within and your Spirit Helpers to work together to turn your burdens into a dance that can then be expressed as joy, so that this joyful emotion can trigger a releasing of stress.

The dance you have just done would have oxygenated your blood and brought energy into your physical body that enlivened and energised you in all ways. See, you are more readily able to smile, laugh, and enjoy yourself. You have just learnt a quick, easy way to shuck off your worries and to fly. And it didn't even hurt, did it?

Now you may ask of yourself, why do I need to do these dances at all? What benefit comes to me if I do this invigorating dance? Is it a waste of time and energy if nothing obvious happens?

Briefly, I will say this: The moment in mankind's history to become aware as a spiritual species is here now, and not in the future or in a long-forgotten past. It is here now, and now, and now. You have little time left for goofing off or wasting your efforts. You have all been round the Circle a time or two and have learnt many things, and it is now time to put what you have learnt into practise. Infinite lives and experiences mean infinite and unlimited learning; you are full to the smallest cell in your makeup of infinite learning. It is time to put it all into use. Simple, isn't it?

Now, you may already know that an uncountable number of books, with mountains of words, have been written on this subject. Countless more will be written on an End of Times scenario for mankind, and the myriad discussion paths that lead to this theorised destination. Of course, each path will have its own multiple directions leading to the final destination with personal idiosyncrasies, much verbosity, intellectual discussions, and as many detours as you wish to take you on a wild ride. But the path to the End of Times is a constructed hypothesis and is not the same as the empowered path towards Home. The paths can meld, but the final destination is different in intensity.

*You can imagine, at this point, a wry shrug of a very influential shoulder and an amused smile, because that imagery is what was floating into my space.*

The dance brings you a renewed energy to see this empowered pathway, to observe where it meanders, with all the twists and turns and surprises it can muster. The increased energy is energy you dance into existence. It raises your vibration sufficiently for you to be able to peek over the wall and give yourself the chance to see the bigger picture. It's like climbing a stepladder to see over the fence to what is beyond. So, what do you do when you are actually in the position to see over the fence? What do you do? How are you to interpret what you see in the bigger panorama? Why? How? What?

# 4

# THE MARCHING FEET OF MANKIND

How...When...Why. Interesting words, are they not? Quite small and easy to say in any language, yet they pack quite a wallop when they are applied to any situation.

I am in the teaching business when I work with these words. This teaching business is becoming increasingly more important, and urgency is creeping into this activity because the Teachers who have been communicating the Spiritual Truths down through the Ages are again stirring, awakening, and becoming readied for the major task of helping prepare for Humanity's immediate future.

How this is done is unlimited and difficult to itemise in any logical manner. The Beloved Ones of, and from, many vibrational levels speak through the hearts and souls of all. Each individual Teacher has their own special ways and means that they can use to communicate with others. Some may prefer to extend their energy into various locales, inter-acting with souls such as I am doing right now with this beloved daughter. The words are dictated and written down onto the paper, and from there the words and ideas are spread out into the community.

Now, still using this specific type of teaching and situation as an example, it is not just the words that are dictated and recorded, because my influence continues in many other ways. I do not write a book then leave the district. Indeed, my energy will remain with the creative process from pen to the reader, and influence many decisions and events along the way. As each person reads my words, my energy will be in their heart, gently interacting and doing what is possible to do, such as to trigger insights, understanding, and new ideas, and bring empowerment into their personal life. In fact, a 'bridging' energy is put into the activity.

Other beloved Ones manifest into the visible physical reality and do what is needed and what is possible to do physically at the time. Others work in the dreaming worlds, the meditative worlds, and the natural worlds. Some work with feelings and emotions, bringing clarity and guidance to whatever needs to be experienced.

These beloved Ones are many—and this generic term means Angels, Helpers, Guides, Saints, Brotherhoods, Guild Members, and so on; in fact, all who use their abilities to directly assist in mankind's ascension to the understanding who and what you all are. Oh, many are we, many, many, many, and before you ask, I will state here and now, there are enough to go around. There are enough Helpers to guarantee all the help you will ever need.

The people who have been born into this timeline of Now are of interest because many of these souls have been born specifically to bring back the Spiritual Teachings to the masses, a time when the tick-tock time is most urgent and chaotic.

Sound familiar? Do the plethora of channelled books and trance messages, prophetic dreams, children's visions, unusual happenings, and healings now begin to make sense?

These teachers who live amongst you are being awoken to their destiny. They are being woken and encouraged to begin spreading the Truth to the world. A huge upswing of spiritual awareness is being lifted into the limelight on the wings of the beloved Ones, and this will continue to happen at a more rapid rate.

The children now being born will bring amongst their numbers some very Advanced Souls who will become well known and of notable stature among you. The wave of teachings is building to a crescendo. The deep, strong work being done by the Light Warriors of your World is slowly increasing this energy wave in strength and density. This power surge is to be used as a base for the Teachers to come, and the Teachers who will continue to emerge into your sphere of activities.

You may ask, 'Why and when does all this happen?'

The when is now. Look about you. And you still need to ask this question? The when has well and truly begun, and it is heading for a massive change of intuitive awareness and understanding on the part of humanity.

*These was such a strong feeling of theatrical disbelief coming through with these words, it was as though Samuel was making a point that we need to start seeing what is right in front of our noses before we go out looking for answers elsewhere. Don't ask questions when we are already being hit over the head with the answers.*

Why?

It is now time for the next evolutionary step to manifest into creativity. The marching feet of mankind are quickly nearing an uplifting step—a step up in intensity of the vibrational energy—and for mankind to be ready to reach upwards safely and surely, this step needs to be negotiated confidently and with trust.

This step of ascension is close. As mankind counts the days, there is little time for the waffling ones and the fence sitters to do anything more than watch the march of humanity move grandly on by. And believe me, the waffling ones will be left behind, because the time to select your destiny is now.

It is time to choose if you want to go Home, or if you do not want to bother expending any energy. The beloved Teachers of all ilks will always lovingly encourage you to raise your head and look above, to see the majesty in a stormy night, to raise your eyes from the ledger and see the God Within, or to respond to the innocent smile of a baby. Open your heart to the Light and take it from there. Just look up and see.

*There was a lot of good humour about; it permeated the room. As I was putting down the words, the energy seemed to increase dramatically and the emotions inside me were strengthened to such a degree I felt like crying with joy. A strong welling up of emotion!*

*Samuel continued to write, although the official book dictation was finished for now. I put down the extra words simply to give you an idea of how the energy can disperse quickly—or how it can, as in this case, stay. My hand was being pushed strongly along until the following had been written.*

Now, that is chapter 4 finished. This is a short one. We do not do headings yet. The words do not come as smoothly for some chapters or sessions. We do not see if one example will suffice. We may need to add more analogies.

Hmm, hmm...

I do write what I wish. You see, dearest daughter, there is a variation in this endeavour that was probable at first, not factual. I monitor this. A creative exercise is one that encounters and encompasses all happenings. A fluid, creative exercise! You are blessed of God, dearest daughter, you work well.

# 5

# THE COOKING POT

At this time, there is a desperate need for the Teachers of Truth to come into the lives of each and every person, in an upfront and personal way. Now, make no mistake with the interpretation here, dear readers. I am talking about the teachers you may see as 'external' to the physical 'you', the ones that seem to come from outside your circle of energy and come flowing into daily life.

In the bigger picture, there are no definite boundaries between souls, or anything else for that matter, and there is no inner–outer, you–them, or over here–over there. I speak of the Teachers who appear to be coming from a different focal point than your own inner core. After all, where the focus is at any given time is the point of interest and power.

These Teachers, who are quietly working away and doing what is possible for them to do to mentor others, are numerous. This I have said, and you know I have already said this. We also see the souls who have reincarnated at this time awakening to their chosen responsibilities. Many are being shaken awake, and at the time of their shaking can go through some traumatic yet exhilarating remembering.

Are you one of these reawakening souls?

Do you see strange symbols floating through your mind? Are words repeating themselves in your mind over and over again? Do you have song lyrics thrumming in your head, lyrics that will not go away? Do you have strange, alien, or Angelic Beings visiting you in your dreamtime?

Has your life suddenly taken a sharp turn away from your comfortable path, and you don't understand why this is happening? Are you becoming dissatisfied with how your life is going? Do you sense you are not doing what you think you should be doing? Are you being pushed by circumstances into a way of living that is different from what your family and friends are doing?

These reawakening people are everywhere ...*huge smile from Samuel...* and you may look no further than your own self to know this is so. As I have said before, each reawakening person will bring into the light different teaching skills, and a wide range of insights.

And insightful people are desperately needed now to help bring enlightenment and understanding about the world events that are causing troubles and woes to the populace. Some people will feel the call or inner urge to write books, not knowing from the start whether these books will be ever published, or indeed even read by anyone other than themselves.

Many times, you will notice that these writings begin or emerge from chaos. The author writes from the depths of despair or writes out thoughts and feelings in an attempt to work out where he or she is going off centre in their life. The act of putting into words the tumbled emotions instantly help bring structure and clarity to what they may perceive to be the incomprehensible situations they find themselves in.

Writing things out is only one way, of course, but in these more modern internet enabled times, every written word has the power to create bigger and faster changes in both the writer personally and potential readers across the globe.

*There was a bit of wry humour here, and it seemed to be connected to and twisting through the word 'modern'.*

The progression of this type of writing can be very influential in structuring and restructuring the belief systems of both the writer and reader. If something stupid is written, then in a later reading it will be seen to be stupid or inane, and a change of thinking may occur. It is a progressive journey of introspection and insight that emerges and then flows out into everyday life events. And as these insights become clearer, the writer and reader will see that signposts also become clearer and point towards a destination of sorts.

All insights, events, and intuitive flashes lead towards awakening the knowledge of whom and what the writer and reader really *are*. Do not think for a second that everybody is just a flesh and blood structure that can move around, touch things, hear things, and when the allotted earth time is done, fade off into the great oblivion. Everyone will need to acknowledge their true identity as an Energy Spark of the Divine, and the physical coat or apparel is a small aspect of the whole.

The physical aspect is truly such a small focus of the Greater Soul or God Spark within, and this physical existence is for learning to create with and to manipulate energy, and to understand the cosmic lessons that are both associated with and stem from this creative energy use. Do you now begin to see the path of remembering what you are here to do?

Once you see that something strange is happening in your life, you are in the position to open up the antennae a little wider than usual, and you have the opportunity and trigger needed to begin asking the questions that need to be asked. And you know that you are able to receive any incoming answers.

If you are serious about listening for answers to your questions, the inner you will automatically awaken the process of remembering the blueprint that was laid down before you were born. This remembering encompasses the awareness of who you really are, and what aspect of reality you have decided to work with in this physical life.

Before birth you had a grand plan designed and possible routes marked out on how these plans may come to fruition. The trouble is, the birth process sends this blueprint and all these plans into a hidden or inner level of vibrational energy within you, and it is only accessed again in bits and pieces as you dip your focus either widely or briefly into this layer.

The plans are never lost; they are always recorded safely and remembered by your inner Soul, so connecting with the God Within is the best and shortest way to recall your plans. As the writer writes of these personal and positive spiritual experiences, he or she puts down a pathway towards their inner landscape, and it is by sharing one's own experiences in this journey to others that both strengthens and spreads the teaching of Truth and Love to the populace.

Each soul has experienced a lot of what it needs to experience already, so will have the firsthand knowledge needed to be able to teach the way to the Truth, with integrity and enthusiasm. It only needs to be remembered.

Now, one Soul may become a Teacher of the Light by writing about their personal inner journey and awakenings. Another may become a Teacher by remembering the way healing energy can be activated and worked with.

You have watched young children playing. One will pick up a stick, then stand to attention and shout that he will be a big General who leads the Army, while another will sit quietly and build a house of leaves, sticks, and mud, or whatever is nearby to work with.

Another will pick up the local cat and stroke it, nurse it, or take burrs from its coat. This child has a natural pull or soul destiny to explore the healing of hearts, minds, and souls in more depth. Or at the very least, has a desire to learn energy usage connected with healing. There may have been a specific reason to choose healing in this current lifetime, maybe to work through some soul lessons that were not understood well enough in a previous turn of the Wheel.

This child will be encouraged to bring into reality what is needed to be understood. In later life, this child may not have a career that will involve the healing arts in any way. That is fine, but if there has not been a physical attempt to understand healing up to this point, deep within there will be a strengthening of restlessness, or an uncomfortable feeling that they are missing out on something, and an inability to put the finger on what it is that bothers them.

There will be plenty of unseen helpers, spiritual guides, angels, totem animals, inner God impulses, and subtle signals aplenty that will continue to point the way to 'healing', but as you all know in the tumble and stress of the daily grind, sometimes not many of these signals and intuitive hunches get into the conscious awareness of the receiver.

It is when the time to open up to these inner urges becomes stronger that the lifestyle path they are currently on, may suddenly become filled with obstacles and detours, making their daily journey difficult. It is when the person begins to ask questions about why these blockages and hiccups are suddenly appearing out of nowhere that the focus or antennae are expanded into newer areas and levels. And hopefully one of these levels is the inner one.

*There was a sense of great humour here in the last sentence, as though a joke had just been uttered. I think Samuel is referring to the scenario, where if something is going to go wrong it will, and this should stimulate people to think about how and why it is going wrong. He has done a sneaky teaching here by coming at a subject he has been already talking about, in a different way. Of course, put out the questions and listen for the answers, then the way always opens into the inner levels. This was what Samuel has repeated since the start of the writing.*

It will be at this time when the healing incidences and events pop into the awareness and day-to-day life of the seeker. Maybe a little animal is hurt and is left on the doorstep, and in caring for this little one, the person remembers the childhood love of nursing and caring for anyone and anything in need.

Maybe they break a leg in a major or minor accident and consequently lie in a hospital bed wondering why this accident happened to them. While there, they have plenty of time to remember their childhood love of healing and helping to fix broken things, and this may be reinforced by watching the hospital staff going about their duties. There will be some sort of trigger that will bring the remembrance of 'healing' back into their daily thoughts. And this all connects with the understanding of what the healing energy really is, where it comes from, and how it is used. This knowing needs to be activated and then shared amongst the populace.

In case you, and you, and you have forgotten, healing energy is Creator Energy, God Energy, Universal Energy; it is All That Exists. Remember?

A healer helps to focus this energy in many ways, but the end result must be the empowerment and enlightenment of the client. The client's Inner Soul knows what is needed and, with loving gratitude, will accept all help to reach this activating level. Remember?

A healer teaches healing by teaching and demonstrating enlightened actions and self-empowerment to others. A good and effective healing teacher will be able to spread these teachings in practical ways that can be understood by even the most obstinate client. Truly, a great teacher can open up dark and gloomy lives as though a light has been turned on. So, are you a teacher of healing or are you in the process of remembering another ancient skill that is desperately needed in this day and age?

Hmm? Hmm?

*It was now a month since the end of the last session. I was ready to take down the dictation, and as the pen moved along the lines, it was as though the last word written a month ago was written a few moments ago.*

Dearest daughter, we are happy to be working with you again.

You may be a teacher, one of the ones I have been talking about, yet you have not woken up to this fact about yourself up to this time in your life. Do you feel this is possible?

*There was a sense of cheeky humour here, and I was now questioning if what Samuel just said was true, because I have always... as long as I can remember...been interested in general healing and general spirit energy 'stuff'.*

*My career choice was nursing. I studied Reiki and did multiple diplomas in natural healing, and so on. But despite all the physical things I have done, I believe Samuel may have been pointing out that the interest may be there, but have I done what I need to do for me personally, or do I truly understand enough to be an effective healer/teacher in the big game of life? This needs more thought. And of course, this is another button being pushed by the Upside Team.*

Each soul has something to share and teach to others. It may not be a deep spiritual teaching, and it may be something as simple as knowing and being able to teach an easy way for people to meditate. Not everyone has the ability to demonstrate to others a comfortable way to sit still and remain silent. Maybe you believe you have no teachable skills, but think about it for a moment, because maybe you knit well. Therefore, it is this skill with needles and yarn that you can teach.

The simple act of knitting brings a stillness of sorts because sharp focus is needed on what is being created with the needles and yarn. The mind is being focused fully (hopefully) on the action, leaving the inner focus and energy free and unfettered. Now, this is a productive time for this inner energy, because as soon as the constant stress of worry and busy thoughts goes elsewhere, the proverbial weights come off and the real work is able to begin.

The Inner You, the unseen you, is an effective powerhouse computer that can do marvellous things. It can solve problems, create new files or insights, and put forth symbols to be seen as route markers. The now unfettered inner self makes the most of this freedom, and invariably the results of this zipping and zapping of energy are insightful, beneficial, and empowering.

When the practice session is over, these amazing insights or lists of directions may not pop automatically into conscious thought because the focus once again is on the day-to-day stress and worry. The stress mode is dominant again. It may not be until the learner knitter is asleep or dozing that the newly arranged thoughts have a chance to float to the surface, so to speak. A child learning to knit is more likely to have a more immediate insightful response to these inner workings because they don't have the depth of 'stuff' to shuffle around.

Alright, that example is probably more a feminine one, but not always, because the male gender has been known to be expert knitters, with skills to weave and to create patterns with thread and yarn.

Allow me to give another example: a young person being shown how to carve images from wood. The same comments from the above paragraph apply to this example also. A steady focus on anything external allows the inner person to work in a less restricted fashion.

By teaching small skills to the previously unskilled, in a very personal way you are teaching a practical approach towards enlightenment, whether you realise this side effect is happening or not. So never feel that you, and you, and you have nothing to contribute to the great teachings. Everyone contributes in one way or another. Everyone, without exception, has the ability to be a sparring partner, a stimulator, or an encourager to others.

And in the Big Cooking Pot of Creation, all the little bits and pieces are thrown in together and stirred and stirred over the broiling energy. What comes out of the pot? Is it palatable? Sometimes it is, sometimes it is not. The issue is not whether it tastes good, but the overall effectiveness of the brew. Does the resulting brew, made up of humankind's input and actions, make an effective and empowering elixir, or is it an unsettling brew that needs more refinement?

A brew is a brew is a brew; a teacher is a teacher is a teacher, and with this same rhythm, a student is a student is a student. They are all in the pot together, all brewing energetically away.

One ingredient can never stand out by itself; it cannot climb out of the brew and cling to the wall of the pot.

It is **all in together**.

Teachers, pupils, everyone together! The pot is brewing. How do you wish the brew to taste? Palatable or unpalatable?

Dearest daughter, this is the end of chapter 5.

# 6

# TALENTED PEOPLE

The teaching of the Truth is everywhere, and everyone has their little speciality niche they know they are good at or are at least competent at doing. Just look around at those close to you—your friends, and the members of your local community—to see if this is so.

And this a general observation because there are such a lot of talented people about. How many people have talents they are too shy to show to others? How many are too busy to come forth into the public eye, or don't want the ensuing scrutiny?

Every person, no matter their occupation, marital status, age, cultural background, and so forth, has teaching skills of one kind or another. This is not an over-the-top statement. Just because you don't know of the hidden talents of others does not mean they do not exist.

As an example, you may look at Mr. White who lives in the next street and notice that he sits under a shady tree and drinks a lot of alcohol, and he does not actively participate in any community affairs. People may think he leads a wasted life, but maybe Mr. White has the ability to read true messages in the clouds.

You may think the alcohol has gone to his head when he comes out with some of the things he says to passers-by, but maybe this man has a real talent for reading cloud formations and cloud messages.

He is not just reading the cloud as a weather forecaster would do, but in a more in-depth and spiritual way. He may see a bear image in a cloud above him and be able to put this formation into a valid message context when he is speaking with someone, and he knows intuitively this is a meaningful message for this specific person he is speaking to. And he also knows this person needs to meditate or 'go within' and do an inner quest to find the answer to a vexing problem that up to this time, he or she has not been able to begin understanding.

Yet would this person believe Mr. White if he spoke openly of what he was seeing and sensing? Bear in mind—and the pun is intended—that the cover of alcoholism puts a sheen of opaqueness over the expressions and events in an alcoholic's life. The alcohol does not remove the innate ability of anyone. It does not act like darkened sunglasses that hide the world from the wearer and the wearer from the world, because for the drinker, nothing is disintegrated and nothing disappears, so nothing is lost. The physical senses may be dulled, but the essential person is alive and well deep inside.

So, what talent does your local alcoholic keep hidden under a fog of inebriety? Can you see beneath this self-imposed shielding? The alcohol usage and the accompanying lifestyle show the intuitive people in the community that the drinker is afraid to use their inner strength and knowledge.

The drinker may feel ostracised because they feel or see things in a different way to other people, and on so many levels is that scary and unsettling. So, the uncertainty is hidden beneath the haze of alcohol and is not dealt with at all.

I suggest looking at each person with new eyes. See deeper than their outer skin, their clothes, and the house they reside within, and see what you can sense about the not obvious energy levels. I am not suggesting that you do an in-depth scan of anyone, but I am suggesting you open up the general senses and see if you can pick up tendrils of information freely given, but at the same time disguised or covertly hidden.

You may know of a man who is a powerhouse of success. Maybe he is a mathematician or a scientist of renown, yet as you look at this person with your 'new eyes' you may see a vision of a flower in his hair. What an incongruous thing to see, but this interesting symbolic vision may indicate to you that this man may have a hidden talent for sensing what flower essences are beneficial and healing for people in need.

Your world is a funny old place where you cannot take anything at face value. Yet this is exactly what you have been brought up to do, isn't it? The trend in most civilised and modern cultures is to firstly judge a person on their outer appearance, and this needs to be changed and changed quickly. Time is running out for people who are still value judging everything by physical looks and monetary success. You need to look under the surface and see more of the true state of things.

Another example: You have a person in your world that for one reason or another you dislike heartily. It does not matter the reason. Maybe you feel they are a snob, an idler, a tattletale, or mean spirited; it could be any one of infinite reasons either logical or illogical why you dislike this person.

Here is what I say to you. You need to look very carefully at the 'underneath' person, and not just the outer appearance. Try and sense how or why the meanness, the spite, the snobbery, or the behaviour that you dislike has emerged into the character of this person. Has this behaviour been there since birth? Is it a reaction or defence shielding against a distressing experience? Look carefully and don't try to get an answer straight away. Put out the question and give your intuition permission to show you the answer.

If is appropriate for you to know, you may find out the reason. Bear in mind that the answer will not be a skin deep, physical reason. Did they have some ability and promise with some empowering skill, yet have been unable to develop it and deep down feels this lack of fulfilment? Does this one fear to be poor or needy? This is quite an interesting exercise to do while you are sitting waiting for a bus, or waiting in a crowded place like a shopping mall or at a crowded beach. You may surprise yourself at the information that flows back to you.

Some of the received information may not make sense to you, but that does not matter. You may be touching into levels of inner knowing that allow you to sense that there is, yes indeed, something different about the targeted person, but you may not need to know exactly what it is.

But if you have received a strong impression, or an impression that seems to be at odds with what the person's looks suggest, don't throw this impression away just because it doesn't seem to fit. Think about it, and then think about how you react to this person. This is indeed an interesting exercise.

Now, if you are trying to intuitively 'read' the person you dislike and you have received some type of impression, it's time to turn the focus towards your own inner self. See why it is, or how it is, that your emotions clash or feel uncomfortable with something the other person is expressing.

Mirror, mirror on the wall, who is the fairest one of all? Did you find you have similar talents or skills on this inner level, similar to this person you dislike? Do you feel uncomfortable that the other person is using, or could use, skills that you know you have but have not bothered to use? Is there more of an internal connection with this person than you would like to admit? This really is a fun exercise to do.

*Samuel was in great humour here, because he was dancing the words around in twisting, tangling and in unexpected interlocking ways. It was fun to feel, and the sense of the ridiculous kept bouncing back into my own thoughts. I could feel and see the words dancing and I think the 'mirror, mirror on the wall' says it all.*

Don't put any limits on what is allowed to come from your inner processes. Find the unexpected in both the disliked or mean-spirited target and yourself! Teach yourself this lesson well. Everyone is not the sum of their public persona. The hidden lives of many people hold most magnificent attributes, and a working teacher of the truth has the ability to help bring this magnificence into the Light.

Therefore, what lessons can the local alcoholic or mean-tempered person bring to your attention? And from these, what insights can you bring back about your current state of affairs?

Lift the lid on ignorance. There is a jewel of knowledge within each and every person, and it would be a waste of resources not to dig just that little bit deeper and uncover the treasure trove within. This digging can be easy to do most of the time; it can be as easy as taking the correct action or speaking the right word at the right time or place. Sounds simple? It is.

The questions you need to ask now are these:

What would you do next? What do you do when you have found a hidden jewel of freely offered information within someone you have intuitively connected with? Do you ignore this insightful information? Do you race over to the individual and blurt out what you sense or think you have found? If you do this, you may have to fend off an unpleasant reaction, especially if you have forgotten to be diplomatic in the way you approach the person.

*There was a big smile hovering in the room, just the smile and nothing else.*

What on Earth is the use of all this new knowledge?

The use is this. You are the one to do something with any new insights about someone's hidden talents. You, only you, because what you have found benefits, or should benefit, you in some manner as another jigsaw piece that will help you sense the total connectedness of All Things. Know in your heart of hearts that there is purpose, application, and inspiration in adding sublime depth to what may appear at the time to be a meaningless and frustrating existence.

These hidden talents are not being unused because whether the owner of these hidden talents realizes it or not, there is a continual sharing of spiritual insights, and teachings, and enlightenment with all others at all times. This may not be on a physical or conscious level, but readers of these words, please believe this: they are being shared in one reality or another.

It is up to you to note your reactions to sensing and finding hidden talents and attributes in other people. See if you feel an affinity for this person when you connect on this level. See if this new information changes how you catalogue this friend or acquaintance in the social hierarchy and ranking.

Do you now see him or her in a different light? If you do
so, it is not because they have changed or altered their lifestyle;
it is because you have changed, and it is this change in your
perception that is important.

See how sneaky all this can be? You have unwittingly found
a teacher who didn't even know they were teaching, yet they
have changed something quite tangible in you, the student of
'life'. Do not condemn anyone thoughtlessly, just open your
perceptions, swivel the antennae about briskly, and instead of
pre-judging anyone, see what you pick up as a gut feeling or
an intuitive response about this person. Learn from your reactions, and not their reactions.

Even with the plethora of Spiritual Teachers travelling the
Earth as I write, don't take all the words and ideas you may
hear as fact, at least, not until you have checked with your
intuition and found how you truly connect with them.

Do they feel right to you, or do they feel to be not quite
right? You don't know? Right? Wrong? Sounds interesting?

A true teacher will give ideas and information to the
audience and then allow each person to come to their own
conclusions about what is being taught. Force or coercion
immediately raises a red flag of warning, and instantaneously
personal defensive walls are erected. Again, it is not the teacher
and the teachings that are of paramount importance. It is your
reaction to them that matters.

Now, as you can surmise, to have every person acting as a
guru is not what I am talking about. Even in more sparsely, as
well as in more densely populated places, you would be overwhelmed with insights if you opened your senses and tried to
espy the hidden teacher in everyone. You would have a brain
blow out!

Instead of putting your brain in danger of overloading with unnecessary information, your canny intuition selects a focus range for you to use. You will be drawn to the people who have the teachings or talents that you need to understand at the time.

The trick is to acknowledge why you are curious enough or empathic enough to try and work out why you are curious about a person, event, thing, or whatever it is in the first place. Am I going around in enough circles for you?

*This was fun. There was such lively humour and a sort of teasing wit coming through with these words. And of course, I had the video playing in my head of multiple curiosities chasing each other around and around, and at the same time being curious about why they were doing this chasing, and why they could not catch each other.*

Have you sat for a moment and twigged that someone else is looking like 'that' right back at you? Are you giving everyone the real impression of you, and are you communicating clearly whatever you are, or want, or need to be?

The watcher watches the watcher watching the watcher!

Circles! Circles! Circles!

# 7

# THE CIRCLES OF LIFE

L et us look closely at where these circles lead. Do they take you around on the same path in a restrictive rut that never goes off track?

Whatever you feel or think about this, remember that the circle represents a Total All That Is—because it represents a balanced whole that encompasses all life directions. And as you finish your first circle and begin another, the path is never going to be the same. Even the donkey harnessed to a millstone will see each circle as a new circle. The feet may be walking on a similar looking path, but it can never be the same one.

As a returning soul, do you go around the same pathways and do the same actions every day? Or do you constantly wear blinkers that only allow you a narrow, local focus? Or do you, as a returning soul, shuck away the ties that anchor you and come freely onto the circular path unfettered and unlimited?

Each life lived has circular motions, with a beginning and an end that ties in with the next beginning. It is the Wheel of Life. It is The Circle of Life. Many wheels and many circles have been there since mankind emerged into the physical aspects of creation. And the circular motion will always bring you back, every time, to whatever it is that you need to experience.

Now, I suggest you look again at your everyday life. What annoying issues keep coming back time and time again to anger and frustrate you? What situation do you always seem to find yourself in? Do you usually choose partners who are less than compatible, or are obviously wrong for you?

These recurring behavioural patterns are in the 'Shadow Circles' that will continue to follow you around until you realise they are there to be seen and acknowledged, therefore connect with them in a positive and empowering manner, and deal with them in an enlightened way. They will remain until you acknowledge their existence and work through the issues they raise in an insightful and practical manner. This is the key to successfully solving any problem. And this you already know.

When these recurring behavioural patterns in the Shadow Circles have been worked through, the shadows are released and the circular way becomes clearer and clearer to see. In the fairness of balance, the circle also has a luminous 'extra' path. The happy souls who have worked towards this brightly lit path will understand in a deep, intuitive way of what I speak.

To have the Luminous Wheel radiating within you shows that you have become empowered working with, and understanding, the transmutation of the Shadow Circle. The words I write in this tome are primarily for the many who have not reached this state of understanding to any effective degree.

*An uplifting energy floods over the desk and surrounds, despite the serious subject matter. I can feel the energy within me strengthening and rising, and I am being shown that this strength and power can be immense and unstoppable! It is as though to some extent we are all battling issues in this Shadow Circle, maybe including Samuel himself. I suggest this because he often includes himself among the many, at points along the way.*

I see your comment, dear one; of course, I am with the 'many'. Few are so highly evolved that there is little work to be done to be considered an Illuminated One. I am, indeed, an earthy one at times and I still have the privilege and pleasure of experiencing many foibles. My many circles of 'life' have been, will be, and still are part of a very comprehensive and stimulating existence. And so, it is with everyone.

Please allow me to digress a little. Not everyone needs to have these problems and mistakes constantly in front of their faces. Every now and again, it is quite acceptable to throw your hands in the air and shout: "I let these problems go! They are too much for me to handle right now. I release them and give them to my Creator to deal with for me!"

Then go out into the fresh air, have a swim at the beach, take a picnic basket into the local park, or have a malted drink with your friends. This giving up control or worry and stress, even for a brief time, can be a very helpful and rewarding activity.

The problems do not always go away, and indeed, if you have a problem with drinking excessive amounts of malted drinks, you may increase the stress. But if this latter one is your problem, then I strongly suggest you go for a swim in the lake or organise the picnic instead.

The little respite from your problem allows the focus, or the Power of Now, to seek out newness, or to catch sight of the chink of light showing through the wall of worry. You can go back to consciously working through your problem with a refreshed outlook, because you see things from a newer and less clouded angle.

This may sound quite simplistic, but even you, and you, and also you, have at one time or another, tried and tried to remember something. The more you try, the further away the answer seems to be. It is when you stop trying to remember and relax that there becomes room in your thoughts for the answer to emerge into, and invariably it does sneak in.

Here is an everyday example…

You are trying to work out why you are always cash poor, or never seem to have quite enough money to pay the bills. This is a good example for you to understand, right? If you are being honest about things, you will eventually realise you cannot blame anyone else for your situation, because it is your personal example and using your personal budget.

Somewhere, as you move around your circle, you have probably created a shadow belief that proclaims 'I don't deserve' abundance, or 'I am not clever enough to handle money', or even 'I do not deserve to have any luck'. Put your own words here instead of the ones I have thought of, because you will know them and they will spring readily to mind.

If you are still being honest, you will acknowledge the fact that you have been thinking or saying these words frequently, reinforcing time and time again the poverty beliefs, not only strengthening them in your thoughts but teaching them to others around you.

This is not a very enlightened thing to be doing: not because of the others, because after all, they may need to work through their own version of poverty beliefs as they move around their own circles, but you keep reinforcing your own belief in your lack of abundance.

Give yourself a break! Go into a quiet place and meditate about why you are always drawn into the same unfulfilling situations that you always fall into. Look at the second last word in the previous sentence. Fall. You don't fall unless you want to fall or agree on some level or another to experience the fall and all it entails.

The act of falling is an act of choice. Like the spiritual seeker or initiate being asked to have faith, and to fly or jump from the cliff. You have all heard this phrase in one form or another. The initiate must choose to move, to fly, or to fall from the cliff before any action takes place.

It is a very conscious or intuitive choice to jump or not. If you don't, you could be standing on the cliff top forever. It is like the young bird learning to fly and deciding to climb onto the branch next to the nest and launch itself into the air.

Therefore, it is your choice to fall or not fall into negative habits or behavioural patterns. It is your choice to deal with the poverty situation we used as an example. The quiet times of meditation will always help you with the understanding of this consequential choosing.

Now, the Shadow Circles don't really care if you transmute them. Transmute simply means a change from one thing to another. Energy is not lost, just altered, so you need to remember that you cannot lose places to put your feet. You will never be left hanging in a void despite the changes and transmutations going on around you.

The main circle will continue despite the shuffling and changing of the pathway components. You don't lose anything but unpleasant or unproductive patterns.

Allow your Circle of Life to shuffle its colours, its vibrations, its signposts, its footpaths, and to help bring an increased awareness and a clearer big picture for you to see what it is you are living through. Arrange for the rainbows to be shown instead of angry storm clouds. Allow for the love vibration to be admitted into the circuitry. Change the way you see your life's path.

Is it stony, rocky, smooth, wet, hot, cold, happy, miserable, or joyful?

If lately there has been a lot of rain in your locale, look to see how you identify with this majestic energy. Do you feel the rain is a nuisance or a blessing?

Think about circles now. See how they link things together. Discover what you are linking together and determine why you have chosen to link every different thing in your life right now, such as situations, people, beliefs, and so forth. Do these chosen links usher you into stressful scenarios, or do they gently link you into empowering situations?

Become a child again and imagine links and circles of all sizes and colours joining everything in your life. Look and see if you actually need all these links. Do you need every one of them to be able to live a fruitful life? Are some links still holding unwanted and unneeded people, as well as outdated stuff tightly into your space? Are some links rusty or needing repair?

Imagine a huge Circle of Life that you are walking along, one with multiple circles or links hooked onto wherever they can attach to, and some are hooked into your emotional circuitry, your physical body, and your belief systems. See unlimited circles, hooked and linked to you as you try to move smoothly around the main circle.

If you have a lot of old and unneeded stuff still attached, it is no wonder you may feel as though you are dragging an anchor that slows you down. Untangle the hooks and discard what is not needed! Allow your Creator to receive these unwanted weights and return them to the Void. Do you understand what

I have said? The imagery is as simple as I can make it. If you do not like my imagery, go ahead and make your own.

*The above book dictation was done three months ago. Much had happened in my life since, with two house moves included.*

*I have now returned to the little flat in the hills where I was living before. After much furniture lifting and shuffling of belongings, huffing up and down hills and stairs and so on, I am at last set up again and ready to resume book dictation. Samuel suggested a time of 8 a.m. each morning to do this and I am happy to oblige.*

*At no time during this shuffling and moving was there an absence of contact with Samuel; it was just not structured for book dictation.*

*The book dictation starts smoothly, as though there has been no time off at all.*

So, the circles are linked in an all-encompassing pattern. You always have a choice of what circles you would prefer to accompany you through the walk of life. Many of these linkages are obvious. Some would be your family, spouse, children, cars, careers, country, ethnic mix, political bias, pets, friends, love of art, and so forth, but what you need to think about now is the invisible, the hidden and hard-to-see links, and hooked circles. For instance, you may be trying to get something specific done and you feel this 'something' or action will bring you lots of money or fame, and so you put your heart and soul into trying to get it right.

Yet despite all the care, the preparations, and all the hard work, the final result finds you in trouble both financially and emotionally. There is no success in any shape or form resulting from this endeavour because circumstances in or out of your control keep putting roadblocks in front of you. The desired result is still a dream; it is still an illusion or beacon that you can still see in your mind but is so frustratingly still out of reach.

Why do you consistently fail to reach this target you are aiming for? Have you thought about this problem in depth, or have you only given it superficial and fleeting attention? Have you delved deeply into the covert meanings why this is continually happening, or tried to work out what it is within you that pushes away this particular dream? Do you feel that it is always someone else's fault and never your own, and this is the true reason you have failed to reach this dream target?

Have you consciously tried to work out any of the overt, and especially the covert, snags that seem to anchor or pull you away from your desired success? I don't mean the in-your-face things but the reasons that are not so obvious and must be lurking somewhere. Despite this searching for them, you have not come up with any logical answers?

Well, dear reader, if this is the case then you may be looking in the wrong areas for answers. Never, ever, is it other people's fault. There is always a reason deep within your personality that holds the key to the true explanation why you don't reach your dream goals. You need to look at the circular path you are now walking along in totality, and not just have a glance here and there. Examine the main path plus the accompanying shadow path, and the accompanying Path of Light. Sense the linkages between these paths and feel or sense where the drag of energy pulls your clarity out of focus.

Take the time to work out where the Path of Light glows and radiates the strongest, and then sense where the darker shadows begin to creep into this Light. These darker shadows can emanate from the Shadow Path or the main Circle where you are at this time.

The hidden shadow links act as delayers, as anchors, and as blindfolds or stumbling blocks of one kind or another. They are not always easy to sense, especially if you do not look at the 'bigger picture' that encompasses your life. If you can narrow the focus to the specific problem of why you cannot reach your wanted target, you can bypass the massive amount of information that is just outside this focal point and can muddle the thinking. By doing this, you gather together all the 'stuff' that you don't need, and you push to one side all unspecific and confusing data that has no bearing on the quest in hand.

Look to the bigger picture, while keeping the question firmly in focus, and you may see in an unrelated area a weird hook or linkage that you can follow back to your current question. This hook is likely to come from an angle that the narrower focus would never have been able to bring to your attention before. You simply could not see it because you were too close, and the extra chaff, stuff, bits and pieces, or old knowledge fuzzed it out. Do you think this claim sounds rather like vague 'New Age' hyperventilation stuff?

It really isn't. The ancient and even primitive cultures of the World had, and still have, a good grasp of this concept and so intuitively spread the searching for answers out into a much larger Circle than you or your neighbours have been taught to do.

*To clarify the above statement a little more: Samuel says there is no difference between what we see as the past, present, and the future, so in the writings it is all called the NOW, unless a specific example is being used as a timeline.*

The modern way of intuitive searching has generally not had free reign to be fully effective, because many people have been taught that whatever happens, it is not their fault. Things that happen to them can be a result of:

God's punishment.

Another person doing something wrong.

Fear of not being strong enough.

Being stopped by the government or council.

Misunderstanding something.

Lack of supplies like pen, paper, money, transport, strength, etc.

And so on, and on, and on, nonstop.

You will understand the situation I am describing, and I guarantee that at one time or another you have used a similar reason. If you find yourself continually falling short of your desired target, make an effort to find out why this is so. If you use your intuitive senses correctly, then you will know that whatever you find will be your priority reason whether it seems to fit or not...and that is fact.

The first thing to do, of course, is to eliminate any simple and practical mismanagement, so check that you are following logical and practical steps to achieve this. After all, this is a physical and practical world you live in, and in this modern day you need business skills or public relationship skills to succeed.

Make sure that all practical and common-sense areas are clear and working to their potential. The next thing to do...if all seems clear yet the obstacles still appear out of the thin air, or if you cannot sense the obstacles clearly, is to go within and intuitively check your circles for hooks and snags. It sounds complicated but is easily done.

Just know that there is a reason for your frustration. If you cannot find the reason after long and involved inner and outer searching in the obvious places, then let the searching stop. Stop trying to find out reasons, stop analysing this and that, and stop stressing out. Say to yourself, "Okay, something is not right, but I cannot put my finger on the reason, so phooey! I'll stop worrying. It's not getting me anywhere!"

Then stop the worry and stress.

Funny this, but as you stop stressing and worrying, you then and only then can begin to get somewhere in your search for answers. Fun, isn't it? To release your focus on trying will release any tension, and this will release the tightly held energy control, thus allowing the escape of your intuitive processes from this stressful control. The inner answering machine now has a chance to sense around the conundrum and see what is really going on.

Allow this to happen. Release stress, concentrated thoughts, and worry, and allow the question mark to float out into unknown areas. So far, it's quite simple, isn't it? Go about your other daily business and give this question mark total freedom to go where it needs to go. It knows the answers to the problem; after all, it has been cooped up in your mind [conscious and unconscious] for quite some time.

*There was such a comical and humorous feeling coming through with the words as they were being written, and a comic strip of many characters was playing out in my mind. There were many questions dancing with glee because they now had their shackles removed and were free to do what they have always been meant to do.*

The now free intuition will flow to where it is drawn to. Don't be tempted to limit anything in any way or shut 'stuff' up in your brain box again. If you feel you are beginning to worry and fuss about a problem, consciously 'let it go' as many times as you have need to let it go.

If you have done all this well, just know in your heart that the answer to the problem will come to you. By preparing, in a symbolic way, you have put out a welcome mat for the incoming answers, and in a practical you way have put up a signpost that says: 'Answer, this is the destination.'

You make a space within your deepest being that allows free passage and helps the communication flow to become effective. You open the doors and put your arms out wide and have a smile on your face that says, 'Welcome'. You expect an answer and wait for its arrival. Simple!

Remember that the anticipated answer may come to you in dreams, in everyday events, hunches, and unusual ways, and you will understand this because we have already spoken of catching incoming messages. Just be aware that the answer to your question [about unreachable targets] may not mention the target question at all, but you will know deep within that there is a direct connection to it when you receive the pertinent insights.

Believe in this information because it comes flowing from the Circle of Light, and it flows across the path you are walking, and sheds Light further into the Shadow Circle. Believe what it says even if this answer is not one you agree with, because it may indicate you are attempting to push into business areas that, in the deepest sense, you are not meant to be in at this time.

In other words, you may be shown quite clearly that you are trying to walk an unproductive path and your Inner God has been doing all it can to stop you jumping into the disastrous frying pan. Maybe you have another business venture about to be offered to you that will be beneficial in all ways.

There will always be a valid soul reason that will try and steer you into empowering action, and it will be invisible until you go looking for it. When the realisation that what you have been striving for is not in your best interests, the invisible becomes the visible, the unseen becomes the seen, and the misunderstood becomes the understood.

The links and circles become clearer. You can release whatever Shadow Circle hook you don't need at this time. Walking the Path of Life is a balancing act between light and shadow. Right now, how many anchors do you drag with you each step you take?

Hmm, hmm, hmm? You see, dear readers, you see? You see? Or not?

This is the end of chapter 7, dearest daughter. A good start. It is indeed a pleasure to be co-creating again. Blessed be.

# 8

# UNSUNG HEROES

You may now think about circles and links, loops, and hooks a little differently than before. The circle is never ending; it continues in all realities, not just on the physical dimensional path where you are at this time.

*A cheeky wave of what can only be described as impish humour seemed to flood the room. This wave was so strong and palpable, and I wished the readers could also feel it. I was curious what was coming next.*

And so, why do I now talk about trees? Circles and trees! This is a wonderful combination indeed.

*Circles and trees? With a chapter heading of 'Unsung Heroes', I didn't expect that.*

A tree is made of circular spirals of energy, the same as you, I, or the rock on the road. The building blocks of life begin in circular movements and continue to move in spiralling movements. The spark of Creation begins, ends, permeates, and is in each and every place you can see, hear, feel, and imagine, and even beyond imagining. There is a common spark that shares with you the entire Universal and Cosmic Lore.

You may or may not be happy to know that you instinc-
tively know a tree in more detail than you feel you need to
know. It does not really matter what you want or do not want;
you indeed have a direct and very personal relationship and
interweaving of energy with the entire world, the planet you
call Earth.

Now the question I ask of you is this:

If you know of this intrinsic linkage, this Oneness, then
why are you hurting, destroying, and polluting yourself?

As long as you ignore or disregard the planetary degrada-
tion that is happening as we talk, you disregard an integral link
and circular connection to your inner wellbeing. You cannot
separate the 'you' from the 'rest'. There is no line drawn anywhere that says Earth only on this side…and you have to stay
on your specific side of this line.

The Earth is visibly in trouble and is about to shake off
some of these irritants that have been imposed upon Her body.
When these events occur, do you think you will be immune
and separate from the ensuing consequences? How can you
possibly be isolated in your own warm and fuzzy cocoon, when
you are a part of Her energy?

You will find your inner cellular energy being shaken and
tossed around also, but deep down, you will know you are trying to rid yourself of self-imposed negatives and trauma. You
'shake' in unison and for similar reasons as your planet.

This shaking…think about this movement, because you are
beginning to see it is already happening. Mother Earth sends
floods, fires, storms, earth tremors, volcanic eruptions, and so
on to wake up and stimulate the vibration of harmony across
the planet and beyond, and to waken the Peaceful Ones from
their inertia.

You give yourself family trauma, health problems, and any variety of misfortunes in an effort to wake you up to the peaceful, loving, innate harmony of the Creator. Can you not hear the alarm bells ringing loud and clear? Have you not heard the cries for help and the begging for aid?

Have you not heard the more enlightened souls amongst you calling for a return to Harmony and Love, in both a personal and planetary arena? Have not you heard?

Here are some examples of the alarm bells that Mother Earth is ringing:

Floods, fires, famines.

Tornadoes, tidal excesses, earth tremors.

Drought, dust, dryness, excessive rain.

Extreme heat or cold, extreme weather patterns, etc.

And so on, infinitum.

Here are some examples of alarm bells you have set ringing:

Emotional upsets, job losses, depression, increase in poverty.

Loved ones in trouble for one reason or another, obstacles, hiccups aplenty.

Feeling victimised in some way.

Feeling powerless at any given time.

And so on, infinitum.

All these and more are alarm bells that are trying to draw your attention to the fact that you, for the moment, have lost the path to empowerment. Therefore, see all calamities in your life as wake up calls. Stop, pause, then react in a way that empowers you, not disempowers you.

For example, you may have lost your job and the rent is due in five days, so do you panic? Get depressed? Rob a bank? Shut yourself in a room? Beg someone else to pay the rent for you? Ignore the due rent? Or do you give yourself the chance to work out that maybe you have another path that you need to walk along?

See every challenge as a beautiful alarm bell that brings to your conscious mind the reminder that this challenge is not doom and gloom but is the most magnificent chance to shake off the negative vibrations around you, thus opening yourself up to miracles. Then follow where your intuition leads you. It is as simple as that. A challenge is a challenge, is a challenge.

Do you now see the reasoning behind my talk of circles and links? This is a graphic explanation of why you need to look after your family and friends and fellow citizens, in fact, everybody and everything in a positive and loving way.

Because how you treat others is exactly as you are treating yourself.

If you cut down a tree, you lop off a part of the inner you, and you leave an imprint or scar in the 'tree' position in your personal energy patterns. This is not a fleeting 'now you see it, and now you don't' type of scar; it is a scar that always stays with you. The only way this scar can be altered is with the energy of the Purest Love in the Universe. This love is able to transmute the frozen energy of the scar and allow it to disperse. Think on this situation a little more.

You may have been watching the news and seeing graphic and bloody video footage, or reading newspapers that show the horrors that mankind in one place or another is doing to others. The unrest and anger are worldwide, and the dreadful actions seem to be getting even more violent and distressing. I now ask you who is being hurt the most? The victims or the perpetrators?

From where I am, I see that the victims have…in a deep, deep level, known and agreed to participate in these actions by taking on the role of a victim. Remember at this point that there are no such things as accidental deaths.

The perpetrators are deeply scarring their soul energy vibrations, and it will take an incredible amount of understanding, self-work, forgiveness, and love, to free themselves from these self-inflicted shackles.

Many of the perpetrators, even when given the opportunities to do so, will never want to become free of these scars and shackles, and they will choose to feel bitter and unloved. What a disastrous present, and what a disastrous future for them. I can think of nothing worse than deliberately misunderstanding the laws of the Creator and feeling hatred beyond logic.

Oh, the despair, the misery, the hopelessness, and the anger. Will you tell me again who the victim is and who is the aggressor?

The angry ones, the terrorists, the fanatics, and the murderers are maiming themselves as much as they damage others. Now, how do you, and you, and you, and yes, even you, help break this negative linkage of hatred, of even more hatred?

This question is one that your world faces now. It is in front of your world face as I write, because there is a strengthening ripple of terrorist activity both physical and political that knows no limits, no restrictions, and no national boundaries, that is already occurring within victimised and disenchanted peoples.

In the older times, the travel was slower, the weapons of a more personal nature—and here I speak of your known history, not the pre-history civilisations. That is another matter altogether. The terrorists and murderers of today's tick-tock time think globally, not locally. So again, how can this negative linkage be dismantled, and all the hatred transmuted? The answer comes in two words:

Loving education.

This is how you break the chain of ignorance and hatred, and unfortunately, the adults will not be as easily helped as the children. The adult terrorists of today have been taught their hatred. The children of tomorrow need to be taught how to love and how to live in total harmony. Remove and isolate the teachers of terror and bring into the schools of learning, the teachers of peace. If this can be instigated in a full and complete way, the world will be a new place and will probably be so within a decade of a saturation point being reached with teaching of the Truth.

This is not an impossible dream, but it will take foresight and immense courage of the people who teach the way of peace in the middle of a war zone. There is always hope that this is possible and effective because there are many brave souls who are doing this courageous action right now. They do not need trumpets and fanfares to tell them they work with God's Angels, as they quietly and effectively go into troubled places where they are needed and plant seeds of hope amongst the turmoil.

You have many, many unsung heroes living and working amongst you, yet you rarely get to read about them. Here is how you can help them, even from your suburban lounge room in a country far, far away.

And please keep in mind when you are reading these words that you have a direct energy connection to both the so-called terrorists and the peace teachers. Focus unwavering on the loving and peaceful feelings; never focus or concentrate on the horrors or damage that is being done by terrorists or like-minded people.

Send your power and energy to the people who are already out there in the battlefields, working with Love and Hope. Strengthen the resolve and effectiveness of these teachers. This is simply done.

Light a candle for peace each day and send a blanket of Light and Love around the Planet. In your mind's eye, see this blanket as a warm, fuzzy comforter that snuggles and surrounds the planet, and sends lovely energy seeping into the hearts and minds of everyone and everything. This also gives the teachers of Hope an extra reserve of energy to tap into, and so helps renew and strengthen their resolve and their sense of purpose.

Meditate. Bring a peaceful state into being. Feel this peaceful state flow to where it is needed.

Send loving thoughts to all the unhappy people. The love and healing may be rejected by some or by many, but even the act of rejection takes focus and energy fleetingly away from the anger and destruction. You can help break the negative concentration, and a chink opens for the peaceful energy to sneak inside the hatred.

Get together with like-minded people, thus compounding the effectiveness of the loving thoughts you all transmit.

Don't focus on the nasty news. Turn the television off, or if you don't want to do this, then put an image of Love and Peace over the screen, knowing that this healing energy will flow back to the events at the point of time they are occurring. This works like a filter that is effective in all directions.

And if you do the following with clarity and good intent, it works effectively and well: You only need to visualise the fuzzy pink around the screen and consciously send it back to the event in a constant loop.

If you do not believe this, think back on a family situation, maybe an event that in the past may have upset you and still bothers you to this day. This event is coloured because of how you remember it, for example, with anger or with sadness, and anything in between. You cannot let it go and continually reset the same emotional trauma over and over again.

Now, go back to this family event and know that when you do, you will see this event in a new way and with new insights. You can now understand the anger and hurt from both sides, because you actually give yourself permission to see the bigger picture surrounding the event. This broadening of the parameters of understanding will trigger a change in how you remember the event. Any positive remembering can bring love and calmness into an unhappy event. And because you focus on it in this way in the present, you bring change to the past. Why not try a quick experimental exercise and broaden your range, and include an everyday situation into the loop?

Give love to whatever or whoever is in the room with you, be it a vase of flowers, a cat, you, or whatever gets your attention. Express this love freely. Love does not have boundaries;

it will continue to flow outwards, inwards and everywhere else. You set the strength of the vibrational energy of love in motion and that's such a good and powerful thing to do.

Follow your intuition; do not pander to your emotions when you think about any atrocities being documented. Emotions unleashed have devastated the Earth in countless ways, and many civilisations before your own have deteriorated because of unfettered emotions.

Get the positive powers pulsing within you, and power up your intuition, because this is your phone line to the Great Creative Knowing. As you watch the dreadful news, push aside your emotions and see what your gut instinct brings forth. You may be in for a shock. You may find out that the people the general viewers perceive to be good guys are also as bloody minded as the bad guys. Knowing this simple fact allows you to have a more balanced viewpoint.

Alright, these are only a few suggestions, but you can see where I am going with them. You have more power to change the world than you realise, and you have more influence in the day-to-day activities than you think. And so, it is timely to practise spreading the blanket of love wherever you like. You will never damage or overdose someone, or a situation, with too much unconditional love.

Whatever you feel, think, emote—from the smallest tear-drop of sadness to the deepest moan of anguish; and from the other side of the equation, from the tiniest smile to the deepest belly laugh flowing from you—all interacts with other people's emanations. You control the personal input into the universal emotional soup.

Put out a linkage made of unconditional love, and it will gravitate and connect with levels of similar energy put out by other people. Think about the phrase 'Like attracts like'. As the love links come together, a chain of love vibration forms and then strengthens. The more linkages there are, the stronger the chain, and as it strengthens this chain becomes a formidable spearhead for peace.

*Spearhead is a war word, Samuel.*

Yes, maybe, but a weapon is only a weapon if the intent behind its usage means war or unloving actions. A spearhead can be a peaceful utensil that pierces the cloud of darkness and horror. A weapon is a tool; it is the intent of the wielder that alters its vibrational molecules.

You have raised an interesting point here and it is one that many forget. You, dearest daughter, immediately thought of the spearhead in the context of war. This is the result of learning, a conditioning of what you have been taught and have absorbed through hours of media rhetoric.

A spear is a shaft with a pointed end and it does not become a weapon until it is used by an aggressor. It may have been manufactured as a weapon, and this title will stay with it, but it will not be activated until the wielder activates it. It can be symbol of peace, a tool for food gathering, pointing the way to destinations, fuel for a warming fire, or even used as a walking stick to help keep balance.

My point here is don't always jump to what seems to be obvious conclusions. There are many layers of meaning attached to each item or thing, and to each and every event that occurs. Look further than the obvious. Again, allow your intuition to work; allow it to bring forth these other layers of meaning. A spear is a spear even when it may or may not be a spear!

*Thanks, I got that message loud and clear.*

Put this lesson towards understanding what your world is going through at this time. Put this lesson towards how you react, and towards what you personally can do in a meaningful and powerful way to bring peace, harmony, and balance into the planetary scenario. Learn this lesson well. Your own salvation is being influenced by how each individual reacts to events.

The obvious is not always what you think it to be. This is a point that I really want you to think about. The conclusions that you immediately jump to comes from the conscious and subliminal learning that you have been exposed to from various sources. The truth may be something entirely different from the obvious, but the real truth can still be accessed easily enough.

Begin by looking under all information that comes your way. Open up your intuition and go with the impressions that come forth. I cannot say this often enough and if you get nothing else from my words, I will be a happy old Spirit.

Let me suggest to you, dear reader, that for one whole day, try to not make decisions based on emotional impulses, and only follow your gut impulses in all things and in all activities. Make it a playful or pretend practice if you feel uncomfortable doing it for real. Pretend it does not matter because you are doing it for a fun exercise.

Now, it is at this early stage you may begin to have the first hint of difficulty and trouble, because most people in the busyness of their lives don't know how to listen to what their intuition is trying to tell them.

It sounds simple and it should be easy to do—indeed, your intuition is a natural ability you have been meant to be using

since birth—but over the years it may have been unintentionally sidelined or blindfolded.

So just relax and try this exercise for the day, but don't
expect miracles and simply have fun with the process. If you
do find that you have trouble working out what your intuition
is trying to tell you, then you know you have work to be done
in letting go of overriding conscious controls. It is not difficult,
but it does need to be done.

Before you begin to clear the intuitive path from control
restrictions, acknowledge the fact that you may have unwittingly put self-imposed blindfolds over your inner intuitive
pathways, and at the same time, you may have voluntarily
given away much of your power of discernment to other people. Begin by acknowledging the fact that you indeed have a
situation in your life that needs to be resolved. Doing this is
always the first step.

Now, over time there have been some great self-empowerment books written, and many more good books will be
written on how you can bring back your personal power, and
open and strengthen your intuitive pathways. If you are an avid
reader, obtain some of these books and follow the advice given
within the covers. Follow the advice that feels right to you.

If you are a 'hearing' person, find out where and when a
suitable seminar is being held and buy a ticket to attend. Or
get an audio copy of the book you are interested in reading.
Find a lecturer who has been through life-altering events,
worked hard to learn the lessons of self-empowerment, and is
willing to share information.

Or simply stay in your own home and begin regular medi-
tations, starting with daily moments of quietness. If you lack
confidence to do anything on your own, maybe go to a class

and learn the different techniques that are available on how to effectively meditate. In a group of beginners, you may not feel as pressured because you are all trying to do something new.

But please remember that you never have to strictly follow other people's formulas for practising meditation. Just do what feels right to you. By all means, note closely any advice given, but ultimately you will settle into your own personal way of doing things. Do whatever it takes to become still and silent.

*There seemed to be a wry and gentle humour over the word 'silent', so was I right in thinking that Samuel has had some interesting early learning times with being 'silent'?*

Listen for the Celestial music only; do not listen to the radio playing, whether it is jazz, popular dirge songs, classical, or rock and roll music. Listen for the heartbeat of the Earth and the Celestial beating of the Drum of Creation. Do not listen to the traffic noise in the background. Just practise being still and silent, because it is in this silence that the inner truths and waves of knowing have the chance to surface.

If you can do this selective listening effectively, you will have done what you can do to take down any restrictive barriers, be they from sounds, emotions, or busy thoughts. You will have opened your Inner Channel. And it is along this Inner Channel that the truths about you and your experiences emerge.

This internal phone connection with the Creative Energy is your intuition at work. The idea is to keep these inner channels open as much as possible as you go about your daily activities.

If this naturally open linkage becomes shut or partially closes, and you want to know the truth about something, then go inwards, remove any obstructions you find, and open the doorway to the place where all questions are answered.

Become so accustomed to doing this opening, and clearing hiccups from the internal phone line, that it becomes a routine part of your existence, a natural part of you that is as natural as breathing in and out.

Here is a little tip on this subject that is not often written or talked about. As you practise your intuitive openings, you automatically open, clear, and strengthen your heart charka energy. You progressively blossom in the loving connection to all that is around you. And as you learn inner truths, you also see and feel more of the loving links that connect to your Universal Others.

You see, just as your foot is attached to your knee, to your hips, to your shoulders, and even to your head, so too is intuition attached to all other parts, and all other aspects of you. And it is not just attachments to you in a personal manner, but connections within your entire unlimited world framework. You blossom like a rose in full bud. And all this majestic stuff is triggered from a little inner quietness. Fantastic, isn't it?

*In the next two days, Samuel gave no book dictation, but the contact was maintained with personal notes for me. These two days were Christmas Eve and Christmas Day, and he reminded me that I was not alone at any time, despite the fact that my own family were thousands of kilometres away. Boxing Day was another matter, and dictation once again began.*

So that you understand why I keep coming back to the basic information, I will repeat this again and again: Mankind's future as a sentient race is in a time of flux. It is like the momentary pause when a person climbs from one rung of the ladder to the rung above. What you do today affects the total outcome of this flux, this next step. Each and every soul, good, bad, or indifferent, has a vital role to play in the outcome.

Does mankind keep the integrity of the Whole, and alight balanced and empowered on the next highest step? Or does the Whole disintegrate, with pieces falling randomly into a chaotic and devastating area? Do only some of the luckier and enlightened pieces reach and achieve safe arrival at the higher step?

A broken Whole is not as powerful as an intact Whole. Therefore, this is a critical time for everyone because the evolutionary ladder is being shaken. You not only have to help with the balancing of this upwards step, but despite the unsteadiness, you need to look up and see where the ladder is being positioned. A determined attitude is needed to stay the positive course as the ladder rungs are navigated. It's having a survival attitude imbued with unconditional love that will be the most successful action, and what is needed to realise your own, and mankind's, potential.

What if you don't like heights or climbing up ladders? What if you are physically incapable of climbing? It doesn't matter; it is not a physical climb we are speaking of here. Mind you, keeping physically fit at whatever level you are able to shows you do know the benefits of health and vitality, and by association this interest flows inwards and affects energy on all levels. This is a win win situation if you have the true meaning of intentional health held firmly in your heart.

The physical aspect is the aspect you see with your eyes, but I speak of the part of you that you see with the Inner Eye. Therefore, anyone—no matter any physical limitations—can join in the metaphorical ladder climb to Home. Indeed, sometimes being physically restricted may bring fewer social distractions, and because of this the focus may already be on important issues.

*Like the being 'silent' comment previously. I think Samuel may know a thing or two about the distractions that can derail the best of intentions, because a loud belly laugh from him at this time pointed to that possibility.*

The climb towards Home has been going for the length of human history, but at various times a natural surge of activity or a stepping, en-masse, closer to the Source occurs. It is a synchronistic movement, like an energy wave that everyone feels. This is such a time and I beg of you, dear reader, to think on this.

Please, please ensure that you keep yourself aware of what is emerging out from the depths of the cupboard and listen with an open mind to what the Teachers of the Truth are saying.

Some of these teachers may have the message a little skewed, but many will not. Listen to them all and pick out the bits and pieces that you feel intuitively are right, and then do something that shows that you understand, or are beginning to understand that you are indeed living in a dramatic time of change for mankind.

Don't be like the lump on the log; instead, be the eagle that soars high and majestically in the Light of the Creator, and by doing so you will reach the next upward step easily and empowered.

Eagles fly, and feathers ruffle.

Eat the chocolate, try the truffle.

Good things come to those that fly

Into the Light of the great Cosmic sky.

Climb the steps, both high and low,

Reach the top

  and

    Take a bow!

# 9

# GET INVOLVED

L et the words fall where they may—for any words you read are simply a printed version of the author's expressed ideas on any given subject, to be used by you to gather helpful information. You have the critical personal energy and choice to bring life and enlightened energy of whatever sort you want, to emanate from the words and opinions expressed.

It is entirely up to you how you react to what you are reading. Do you throw the book down in disgust because you think the author is blatantly against, or perhaps overly for, any specific thing? Or perhaps the author writes some things that you disagree with vehemently; maybe the writer comes through as a doomsday predictor and is dogmatic in an unrelenting way. And on the other side of the equation, maybe the words are so sickly sweet and unrealistic that they are nauseating.

Even if you agree with many of the written ideas, do you throw the book away because of the workload involved should you do the suggested activities within? Does the book suggest even more work come into your life, or load more self-responsibility onto your shoulders than you will feel comfortable with?

Do you read the book avidly, agree with what is being said and why, and can even talk about it with your friends, yet you still make no personal effort to carry out any of the exercises and the various suggested practices that are scattered throughout the pages?

The long and short of it all is this: It is only you, you who can change your world. To implement suggestions or not is the powerful choice you need to make for yourself. Words are words are words, only if nothing is done to connect with them.

Now, as you all know, words can be one dimensional or not. They can be seen as flat, curved, or straight marks on a parchment, paper, stone, earth, or any surface that can be marked. This one-dimensional view is the first impression most people have. But I ask you to see them, read them, and then put the intrinsic meaning of the sentences into the pot and stir it all a little.

Then add the unseen layers of meaning into the pot, and thoroughly stir in the rest of the ingredients. Only when you have done these actions is it time to put the implied world energy around you—the past, present, and future of the surrounding vibrational spaces—into the pot and stir the whole brew. Stir it a lot! Now you are getting into the truer meaning of what you are 'reading'.

For example, behind the given insights and advice, all the earnest urgings, and the emotions you may sense coming from me and my written words, there is a vast background of 'history' and 'teachings' from the Universal Schools of Knowledge that I connect with. I do not spring from the clouds and blurt out simple homilies that I make up on the spot. I draw on a massive and unlimited source of Creative information, and I also put into the brew a big piece of personal history and lessons learnt from the experiences I have lived through. And so, you see before you my interpretation of this Divine Knowledge.

You are being given the key to access the Halls of Knowledge for yourself, so you can interpret this knowledge in your own personal way. Only you can have your own individual slant on how you perceive things. I draw your attention to this now because I need you to understand this point clearly and strongly. Angels can sit on a mountain top and spout about Universal Laws until their wings fall off, but it would be a meaningless exercise if no one really listens or at least thinks fleetingly about what is being suggested.

*A sense of gentle humour and a cheesy smile floated over the pages, and in the comic strip of Samuel, there were Angels sitting on mountain tops checking to make sure their wings are secure and in no danger of falling off.*

You can read mountains of spiritual self-help books, but it is your prerogative to choose not to practise any of the exercises and practical tips that are given within the pages. You may end up a very knowledgeable and theoretical guru, a guru who is very well spoken on many subjects, but until you actively interact with the knowledge gained you remain a bystander, a spectator. And spectators get left behind when the Bus of Life Experience rolls on by.

Are you beginning to understand fully what I say to you? Get involved! Get involved! Get involved! Get involved even if your involvement comes from advice written in an anti-action book, a book written to shoot down everything that you agree or disagree with. Take up a pen and write down your thoughts. Make up your own quiet time routines.

DO SOMETHING!

DO SOMETHING!

PROVE ME WRONG!

OR PROVE ME RIGHT!

Prove me wrong or prove me right. It doesn't matter which or what you prove, as long as you have done one or the other, because to begin this journey of investigation means you begin a wonderful journey of personal enlightenment. Curiosity and involved interest can take the seeker, the re-searcher, the student of life, to link powerfully with the Glory of the Creator. Re-searcher is the word I prefer to use, because it implies that you have done some searching previously into the World of Universal Knowledge.

Applied curiosity opens wider the pathways to the empowerment within. And it all begins from a reaction to your actions, a reaction from you, so in effect you set up a reaction to your reaction.

Do you disagree with my words and the way I express them? If so, then I dare you to write out your own ideas, write out your insights, thoughts, or imaginative short stories, and allow the pen to flow and record words that seem outside the normally acceptable paradigms. Do it—and learn from the experience.

*Humorous strands of swirling, dancing energy were seeping vibrantly through the writing, and Samuel seemed interested to see if anyone would respond to his prodding and needling words. Would there be action, a reaction, or neither?*

All I wish is for you to have a positive reaction to my words, and in this case 'positive' covers either positive or negative emotional triggers or concepts.

You see, dear reader, when you begin to see the bigger picture, you will get a glimmer of what I am talking about, and you will understand that my forceful warnings are not out of place, and that mankind is indeed trying to balance on a huge wave that is rushing towards the rocks. It is a wave with a most powerful force, and you will need to somehow balance on this wave, and then choose to jump on your surfboard and start paddling strongly, or maybe body surf to the safety of the beach.

Do nothing and you will get dumped by the surging waves of energy.

Maybe my words are not written as diplomatically as some others are, yet who will really worry about that when you are in a sink or swim situation? To have someone shouting at you, "Swim! Move your arms and legs! Swim over here!" will be accepted for what it is: help from someone who has your best interests at heart, even if this help comes from someone unknown to you.

Maybe you cannot swim? It doesn't matter. When the adrenalin rush kicks in, you will be swimming and will probably manage to do it quite well.

*Fun imagery swam into the movie theatre behind my eyelids. There were swirls of humour twisting in with Samuel's descriptive words, and I also saw a crowd of non-swimmers suddenly realising they can swim if they have to, and they were so energised and enthusiastic to keep going despite all the flotsam and jetsam that surrounded them in the waves.*

So, words are words, are words, and it is your prerogative to read them and believe them, disbelieve them, or whatever. Now, you may tell me you cannot read, or you know people who, for whatever the reason, cannot read either. And in fact, there are many people who cannot read the written word, so what happens to the majority when large groups cannot read? It doesn't matter whether they can read words or not, they will be given the Message of Hope in one way or another and in such a way that that everyone individually will understand.

We have spoken of this Message of Hope earlier. It is time to give thanks to the Creator for giving each person the ability to connect with and bless the Divine Spark. By using this connection, you strengthen the Flame Within, and you bring the Light into your darkest corners. You give power to you; you bring Light into your life. Oh, joyous is the Soul who dares to do this!

*There was such strong emotion being expressed that it was palatable, and massive goosebumps rose on my head and arms! It was so powerful and moving.*

I can be more biblical or less biblical. I can be anything or anybody, and as long as I get reactions from you, I will be a happy Spirit! A happy Prophet! A happy Messenger!

You may not know this, but at one time or another you all have been through similar experiences. By this I mean each of you have been, at one time or another, in the position of Herald, a working messenger. Therefore, you will understand the satisfaction of delivering a message clearly and well, and especially one that achieves the desired results. Ah, the joys of clear communication.

Be aware that we pause for a brief time. Good day to you, dearest daughter.

*I was a bit surprised at what was said because I felt there was more to be written. I was enjoying this book writing.*

*There were more personal suggestions about what Samuel would like to see get done with the work so far. But it would be another four weeks before Samuel continued with his book dictation.*

*This next book recording session arrived as I was doing the early morning writing in my daily journal; the wavy signature of Samuel was written, and the energy in the place 'changed', so I knew we were back in 'recording the book' business again.*

*The words were: "Samuel here, dearest daughter, put out a new sheet of paper."*

*I did this and the next words in the manuscript were written.*

# 10

# THE BLANKET OF HOPE

You are ready?
*Yes.*

Then away we go; these next comments may end up else-where, but that does not matter. I have repeatedly told you that it is time for mankind to choose which way the collective of the species needs and wants to go. This is a dire warning and cannot be emphasised enough.

I pointed out many pitfalls associated about what is happening and gave some simple exercises and insightful advice that will help even the most uninformed of people, giving them a chance to connect with these choices in a relatively painless way. In these next sessions I will offer more proactive and positive ways in which anyone can be a part of this magical milestone in mankind's history.

The following insights and actions are not new ideas, or even old ones for that matter. They have always been in existence somewhere or other. They are the universal impulses that you are tapping into, with some people connecting with them more comprehensively than other people. Often it is the people who have had lifechanging or traumatic events that triggered the 'learning how to cope' mechanism, or the people practicing meditation and so forth, who are the ones quickly grasping the fact that these Truths are the cornerstones of Life itself. And these Truths need to be expressed freely in both a personal, national, and global manner.

If you understand this specific insight about universal truths being the cornerstone of life, and have the freedom and confidence to express them, you should also understand fully that this is the perfect time for pertinent choices to be made. Actually, you may understand the general situation well, but as you struggle to work out your personal priorities, you may find that the directions are blurry and difficult to see with any clarity because of situations that may not be within your immediate control. You could be unsure of what the better options are, and despite good intentions and a commitment to universal ideals, you still may not have all the needed facts before you.

However, it is not all doom and gloom just because I have inferred that it may be so. Indeed, the truth is just the opposite to doom and gloom. You see, there is more than a glimmer of light hovering over, and into, your box of choices. Many people take the trouble to expend personal energy to peek into this box and then rummage amongst the choices on offer to work out 'what means what'.

How many of these curious and industrious ones do you think there are? A few thousand people scattered here and there? Or one here and one over there, scattered singularly amongst the multitudes? Let me tell you, and this is the truth I speak.

There are multitudes that work with the Light.

Multitudes amongst multitudes!

There are enough of these wonderful people living in each country or division of your planet, who when working together as a whole, can shift the direction and alter the outcome of all actions that are in progress right now, have been, or will be activated sometime in the future.

This is very important, and it cannot be stressed enough. Mankind already has the critical mass of Light Workers to influence the final destination.

Will I repeat this?

*A sort of cheeky humour came through with the last four words. It was obviously a gentle poke at Samuel's willingness to repeat things as often as needed. He will gleefully offer repetition upon repetition, with added pointers.*

This is the Hope, and the reason for all the current intervention and assistance or whatever you want to call it, from your friends and helpers who reside in other dimensions. Please always keep in mind that whatever happens to mankind will impact all these other dimensions; therefore, it is in everyone's interest to work with the Cosmic Laws of Life to ensure that an empowering result ripples through not only your dimension, but all other dimensions as well. There is Hope, beautiful Hope.

Hope and Home. Home and Hope.

It has a musical ring to it, don't you agree?

*I loved this work! As Samuel dictated the words about musical notes, different signs and symbols flashed over the page and danced with glee and energy. Various shapes and sizes seemed to appear and flash over the page, all emitting good humour and joyous feelings in an uplifting tempo. I felt like getting up and dancing.*

I will explain in greater detail how this empowering work is being done in all areas of the planet, and how we all communicate in this tick-tock time of today. You may not be aware of the many in-depth ways that are being activated and used collectively by the Light Workers of the world right now. You may or may not believe anything of this sort is happening.

Usually, it is the people and personalities who thrust themselves into power or influence over the public who generally need publicity to help feed the basic nature of their actions. If the crafted publicity hype is believable, the actual public frequently loses both individual and group power.

On the flipside, the people who empower others do not need publicity unless it is for a specific and helpful reason. I am generalising here because there are always exceptions to every rule, so I put this comment in here to be fair to both sides of the publicity scramble. Look at your current media coverage and look at the news stories from the viewpoint I have just stated. You will not be able to say that I speak falsely.

Check out all my words; do not take them as gospel without checking on their validity. Do your homework. The empowering Light Workers in all cultures go quietly about their business, and their actions are judged by the results of what they instigate and accomplish.

In your day-to-day life, you may miss the news of these quiet Light Workers who go about their business without the fanfare of publicity. And even if you see a positive result from something appearing in the media, it is often the case that one of the publicity hungry ones will grab the credit for the success or somehow insert their profile into the mix. This is not an uncommon practice, not uncommon at all.

How do you find out about these hard to spot Light Workers? How do you begin to look for something when you are not sure of the wordage, the imagery, and the specific definitions for any sort of query? You are unlikely to find the word 'Light Worker' in the form I speak of, in the normal dictionaries and electronic libraries. So how do you begin searching for this very specific needle in the proverbial haystack?

Well, dear readers, if you wish to find out more about the people in your world who are gathering to tip the balance from hopelessness into hope for mankind—or if you wish to locate these people already working in this field of godly love, then read on. I may be able to stimulate your senses and strengthen the hope for mankind and for better times that is already within in your heart.

I encourage you to strengthen the incentive to get to work, and to encourage your personal power pack to move mountains, to walk amongst the Stars, to heal a sick animal, to walk amongst the trees and know what they are saying to you, and most importantly, to use your positivity to tip the seesaw of mankind's journey and into the Light of Unconditional Love.

Are you game? Are you ready, or not?

*This was the end of the morning's book dictation. It was a rather interesting session because of the uplifting energy that filled the room. Samuel always brings such an individual and powerful strength into our contacts, yet it is the feeling of a good friend visiting, a true friend with a comforting and exhilarating energy.*

The 'Hope' of mankind is a tenuous ideology, so what exactly does this word represent, and what does it mean to you?

*The Wordsworth Concise English dictionary: hope to cherish a desire of good with the expectation of fulfilment/ to have confidence in a successful outcome.*

We see 'Hope' in a larger context than just as an expectation of success. It is a tangible, vibrating feeling that can be seen, felt, and heard by you and everyone else. It is a state of 'being', a state of 'doing', and a state of 'happening', and it is already in action and powerful beyond measure.

Hope takes precedence over gloom, sadness, trauma, anger, bitterness, and more. Hope takes precedence over all of what you may think of as negative emotions. Hope is a very tangible higher vibrational energy and is measurable. It lives towards the higher end of the scale. I describe it in this way so that you may put an image into your thoughts, an image that you can be able to correlate with childhood learning of up [Heaven] for good, and down [Hell] for bad. It is really an illusionary yard-stick, but one that may be familiar, so I will also use it for now.

Hope is good. Hope is Heaven, and Hopeless is Hell. Now, have you grasped this distinction in the way I mean it to be grasped? Very good. Now, tear that image distinction up and cast the pieces into the rubbish bin, because the higher vibra-tional energies interpenetrate all lower vibrational energies, and by following this truth, you will need to acknowledge that even gloom and sadness is intermingled with hope.

There is an intermingling of all vibrations that you cannot separate into separate emotions; therefore hope, because of its more powerful, finer movements, will dominate any mixture. Do you understand this? I can go another step and say Love, the vibration of true Love, intermingles with all mixtures and is the higher Energy at all times.

When it is explained like this, you have to wonder why there is so much angst, anger, killing, and hostility in the world today. If Hope and Love are so powerful and are an intrin-sic part of this hostility and anger, why don't they control the lower vibrational emotions? Why do angry people seem to have no 'hope' despite it being a major element in the mix of their motions? Why? Why? Why?

You have seen media coverage of these fanatical ones who want to kill, to maim, and even their own families are not safe from the slaughter. You have seen the results of generation after generation of family feuding, with total families and communities locked into conflict, and a continuation of 'pay back' that leaves no hope for any new generation to break the cycle of hatred and revenge.

These situations can be seen in all countries, in one place and in one time or another, and they can be found without having to look too deeply. So why doesn't the 'hope' part of the mixture do something to break this cycle?

It is quite simple really. Hope will be let loose only when it is able and free to do so. Of course, these fanatics and feuding families know they can stop the rot if they want to. But the force of their teachings, the indoctrinations, and the habitual rut and lifestyle choices block the emergence of hope.

It is a person's free will and personal choices that govern their behaviour. The terrorists, or the feuding families, can stop the hostilities in a heartbeat if they choose to do so. This is the power of the individual, and all the individual needs to do is to remember that a sliver of hope is always within the emotional mixture, then activate this sliver.

Think on this in another way. Imagine layers and layers of different energies, all different levels with different kinds of emotions being wrapped around the wonderful planet you call Earth. There are multiple layers all lined up, layers of hope, love, jealousy, laughter, depression, and so forth, like layers of an onion.

These layers totally blanket the globe, layers over layers over layers permeating all other layers—and then even more. Imagine you are walking in your local area, your feet thumping into the ground, and as you walk, you move through these invisible layers of energy. They brush by you and flow through you like a wispy fog on a winter's morning. You sense them there, and maybe even feel the touch of a misty tendril now and again, but you don't really see anything. This mist ebbs and flows around your movements, dancing and moving to a beat you cannot hear. Yet this misty layer is a very powerful mist because you are able to connect with bits and pieces of these layers.

All you need to do is to focus on the specific energy that you are interested in. So now you have this picture in your mind of walking through a misty, moving fog of many layers, and some levels or vibrations are weaker or stronger than others. You may be able to sense this. For instance, you may feel as though you are brushing though a warm spot, a funny spot, a cool spot, and maybe even a spooky spot. Actually, a 'spooky spot' sounds fun to say; say it fast three times and you will smile at the rhythmic timing. You will notice some differences in the atmospheric feel as you go for the walk.

Here, we have this blanket of many emotions and energies cocooning the World. Why not decide to focus on the part of this multi-layered blanket called Hope and, while you are at it, focus on the Love layer as well. When you bring your focus to these levels, you drop away the hostility, the anger, and the frustrations, and this allows you to concentrate on what you are seeing and sensing on these levels. And you begin to see how bright, how joyful, and how strong these levels really are.

You will begin sensing how people all around the planet are working with and focusing on the Light, all working to keep these levels shining, clear, and strong. You immediately connect with all believers and workers of the Light when you link with this Light. It is like plugging a cord into a vast vat of Light, Love, and Learning. It is like phoning one number and immediately connecting to a worldwide network of like-minded people. And the Light allows the clarity of vision to improve, not diminish.

As more people decide to focus on Hope, Love, and Light, the stronger and stronger these specific misty bands of energy around the planet react. They strengthen and pulsate with their vibrant creative energy, reaching out further and further into the surrounding layers.

As this continues, it is more difficult for the angry ones to dismiss and deliberately ignore these pulsations. In fact, the angry ones will have a curious reaction; they will want to push this pulsating light away, and they will become even angrier and more belligerent. They will want their own emotions of pain and ignorance to 'win'. They will feel threatened.

Liken this scenario to an angry child lashing out at its mother when she wants to put it to bed, and the child is throwing a tantrum because he or she does not want to go to bed. However, ask yourself this: Who eventually wins that specific battle of wills? It should be the mother, but even I have been human enough to know that this is not always so.

*A lot of humour abounded, and there was a strong impression of many, many games being played with varying results that floated with the words onto the page. There was a big goofy smile and good-humoured teasing going on here, and I'm sure the teasing was intended for everyone who has been in situations like this one.*

As with Hope and Love, the mother should eventually win this battle of wills.

Now, what is the most efficient way to connect into this band of Hope that I say is always within you and your surrounds? The easy answer is to just decide to connect with it. Just do it. There is no intricate ritual you need go through, nor a complicated mantra to chant. And a start can be as simple as making a conscious effort to smile more often, or take deep breaths and release all tension on the out breath. It's as simple as ringing a neighbour and saying 'hello', or as basic as helping an old or infirm person to safely cross a busy street.

You can begin by doing the smallest action—because once you have decided, you have already done it. You have focused on the Hope, and you have allowed a connection with your heart.

To reinforce this connection, do the little examples suggested previously, or make up your own small and powerful action. Light a peace candle, plant a tree, wash someone's clothes for them, paint a picture with beautiful colours, give someone who is thirsty a cool refreshing drink of water.

Do you see what you are doing when you do these little affirmative actions? Your focus or concentration goes from your mind's busyness, from your emotional troubles, away from the anger and pain in your heart, and goes into the Light, Love, and Hope mode. You take the controlling and limiting barriers away and this allows the higher vibrational energies to flow into your heart and mind. I do not say your soul here, because these attributes are already an intrinsic part of your Core Being.

So, here is the key. Just open up your heart and the Love, Light, and Hope energy will further strengthen and blossom spectacularly, and it won't hurt a bit!

As you may surmise, perpetually angry people have closed their hearts and minds to Hope, Love, and Light, and consciously or unconsciously continue to block it from emerging into action. To move from hatred to tolerance and kindness, they need to deliberately change their way of life and their way of thinking to allow their walls to come down, thus empowering the connection to the vibration of Hope. Instigate a slight change in lifetime teachings and patterning to see the world with different eyes!

This scenario of hatred is a frightening prospect because many prefer 'death' to a change of daily routines and circumstances. These people are often indoctrinated and afraid, and they need compassion and understanding for why they act as they do.

However, all is not lost. Go into the layers of Hope, Light, and Love, and work with what you have to strengthen and empower yourself and those around you. Eventually, the bands of Hope, Light, and Love around the planet will grow so strong and become so empowering that these people, too, will have the balance and the momentum to overcome the barriers erected by their renegade hearts.

Each Light Worker makes an impact, a powerful impact, and never feel this is not the truth. This impact increases exponentially as more people connect with the Universal network, and work with and share their belief in the Hope, Light, and Love blanket of good vibrations.

During the current time in mankind's evolutionary movement, this band of Light around the Globe is strengthening. You may not sense this power increase happening from an individualistic situation, but collectively this band of Light is bubbling to a crescendo.

More people want and believe in a peaceful existence than those who prefer a disruptive existence. So I urge each one of you to do what you can to help strengthen this collective belief in Hope, Love, and Light, so that it becomes strong enough to rip the blindfolds from the self-blinded, to shake the leg shackles from the ones who feel fettered, to pull the blanket aside from the ones who are hiding beneath it, to make sorrow turn to gladness, to make tears turn into laughter, and to help teachers feel the Truth in their teachings and not just recycle man-made interpretations and dogma.

Help build this global blanket of Light into a layer of protective Love so strong that the hurting, fearful, and destructive people will feel comfort, and the angry ones will come to feel peace. This is beginning to happen as more people in different places around the World begin to look for answers, the answers to why they live in troubled times.

There is a huge surge of energy emerging; it's a massive tidal wave of people beginning the search for answers, and because of this searching they are finding other like-minded souls. And it is this searching, finding, and bringing together of Light Workers that brings this unstoppable and uplifting surge of energy to strength and empowerment.

So how do you begin to look for this like-minded energy manifestation? How do you begin to search for something you don't know much about? You just read on, dear reader. You are already finding some basic answers by reading this book, or the many similar books freely available. Read on and I will give you even more ideas on how you can use your inner talents to help in the survival and evolution of your species.

*There are a lot of capital letters used in the above chapter. These are Samuel's words, and he used the capitals to stress the importance of his message. This is a 'strange' chapter in a way because Samuel was talking about a subject he knows many people will possibly disagree with, and he was trying to put his thoughts across without offending anyone.*

*What I get from these words is that to change anything profoundly only needs a small action or positive thought, and not necessarily a massive change of behaviour, because the smallest of kindly actions can trigger a connection to a much larger band of like-minded people.*

# 11

# CHARITY

G ood morning, dearest daughter. Indeed, I am here. I have never not been here.

*This was an answer to my question of whether Samuel was 'here' and ready to start book dictation. I usually feel the bow wave of energy that comes with the entrance of Samuel, but this time I knew Samuel was in the building so to speak, but I didn't get that the dictation was about to start. There seemed to be good humour and a fun feeling permeating the room.*

Yes, put down the new heading; we are ready for action.

At one time or another, you may think to yourself that there must be a better way to live. And as you look around, you can see other people going through similar life predicaments to you. After all, the media outlets show a continuous stream of good people going through hard times, or desperate, lost, and traumatised peoples in all parts of the globe struggling to live meaningful lives. Some of these desperate situations seem to be triggered by events that people have little or no control over, so they appear to be victims of an angry Mother Nature, or victims of politically ambitious leaders, and so on infinitum.

Why, even the reader who lives in a comfortable home will feel, at one time or another, victimised by the system of government controlling the populace. But even the benevolent governments are stripping away, layer by layer, little piece by little piece, your freedoms, liberties, and power. These restrictions may be as simple as a change in traffic laws, or restrictions on how you look after your pet. The accumulative effect of these nit-picking restrictions can add up to frustrations that are difficult to manage. You will have heard your neighbours—yes, even yourself and family members occasionally say that these types of restrictions have gone too far. Of this I have no doubt.

It is when you get angry and frustrated enough to shout, "There must be a better way!" that the mind opens to the possibility of a better way actually being available.

This is the time when the glimmer of new revelations and insights awaken, and you begin to think that there is a chance to get out of the dark and unsettling places and into the places of positive action. You see, if you are in a comfortable job, live in a comfortable home, or go back and forth along a comfortable rut, you may not have the incentive to open up to change of any sort.

Now, don't jump ahead of the sentence and misinterpret these words. I do not imply that all people who live in comfortable circumstances are in a rut; far from it.

Many of these Souls may have rich and adventurous lives that continually lead to insights and personal growth. These people have already understood that their physical possessions and way of life is just that...a 'way'...and so use this 'way' as a signpost in the journey of life.

These people may already have begun their spiritual journey Home and will continue to do so. But let me tell you, there are not as many of these 'in a comfortable rut but still learning cosmic truths' people as you would imagine.

Being in a comfortable rut makes an individual usually very reluctant to step outside these parameters of safety and into unknown and uncomfortable terrain. Even the people who are on their Spiritual questing and doing well may have imposed comfortable limits to their learning, so the scare factor does not kick in too strongly and shake up their world. They learn and grow at their own pace. They allow themselves to only go to the limits that feel unthreatening.

You see, ingrained habits can be very strong and controlling and it takes tremendous willpower to effect change in behavioural thought and action patterns. Or conversely, only a smidgeon of Inner Power.

In most people, the physical act of stepping out of their comfort zone brings to the surface untold thoughts, emotions, and fears of the great unknown, worries, excitement, and unbalance, plus everything in between. Again, there are the exceptions because many people are so balanced and centred that they can step out into newness and remain strong and balanced despite turmoil going on around them. These are the people who have already understood that the base of power is inside them, not outside and apart from them.

This inner strength and balance become so strong that nothing rocks their equilibrium. There are people like this around you, and you will find them by the energy of Love and Empowerment that they emit at all times. Let me reiterate now, I do not personally advise against living in a comfortable manner.

*There was lots of humour here, like a chortle or two echoing around the room. It was as though there was a secret joke of some sort going on, or Samuel was making a gentle dig at himself.*

But I do advise anyone in these unchallenging circumstances to become aware of any feelings of being blasé, of
being non-interactive in the bigger picture, because of any lack
of interest and stimulation. Being blasé and developing tunnel
vision is an insidious condition that creeps silently into the
lives of even the most contented people.

These are the ones who can watch a documentary about,
let us say for example, a famine in a certain country, or a mas-
sacre of a tribe by a despot in some far away jungle. They feel
compassion and distress, but they do not connect to the action
in a big picture way. It is a surface emotional connection to the
news story and they definitely feel emotional stress, but they
fail to dig deeper or intuit the real reason why these events are
happening.

I am not talking here of a person watching this distressing
film or documentary and then verbally blaming the bad guys, a
government, or some other person who has caused this calam-
ity, and does nothing more. I am now talking about the viewer
who tries to use their intuition to tune into the deeper reasons
why these events are happening in the first place, and why it is
happening in this specific timeline.

And after the viewer thinks about it and partially under-
stands the big picture, they try to do something helpful to
bring a loving energy and balance to these scenarios.

For example, you may see a news clip about famine devastating a region, and feel sorry for the featured hungry child,
and as a result of this empathy, you send a monetary or food
donation to the charity that highlighted the problems in the
drought-stricken country. This action may make you feel
good, but why not go that one step deeper and see deeper

into the bigger picture why this starvation scenario is happening at all?

It is only when you begin focusing on the real 'big picture' reasons that you and other good Samaritans will begin to get to grips with, and have a greater understanding on, how to truly help this hungry child.

In other words, you will understand how to give your help in a more powerful and meaningful way. You will need to step outside the suggested comfort zone of conventional thinking to gain this comprehensive understanding. And you will need to look further than the 'hungry child' image. For example, don't take the offered image as the yardstick on the harshness of the famine; go that extra step and work out for yourself what is not being shown.

See what you can intuit about the politics of the region, the land care and farming practices, or the time aspect of the famine. There is a lot more information to be found than just the name and community of the 'hungry child'. The charities looking for donations will go with the obvious image, but there is always a great deal more to be seen. It is easier for the established charities to use effective standard images that can be quickly set in motion, because the guidelines are already tested regarding viewer response.

You will need to have a reaction that goes deeper than the charity in question expects you to have. The set rules and regulations on how to donate are usually shown to you in the charity's contact information, but these worthy bodies have their own agenda despite what is being made known to you. You hear and see only what they feel is in your best interest to see and hear. By delving into the true bigger picture, you begin thinking for yourself, and this is a very empowering action.

Have I shocked you about my comments on Good Samaritan charities? I hope not because these worthy organisations do a lot of good by the standards they judge themselves by, and in truth, are judged by others. But I repeat, each organisation as a whole may have a corporate agenda to fulfil that may not be known to the individual volunteers or even some personnel in the corporate body of any given organisation.

Again, look at the bigger picture. There may be a perceived gap between the reality of a starving child who is hungry because of man-wrought political corruption, droughts and food shortages, and the volunteer or donor who lives in comfortable circumstances but who gives time and energy to the 'poor' for personal reasons. But as I have previously said, nothing is in isolation, everything and everyone is intrinsically linked. There is no gap.

However, maybe it seems the right thing to do because helping makes the volunteer feel warm and worthy. Maybe the preacher suggested it, or working as a volunteer takes away some boredom. Maybe you are good hearted and want to help. There are uncountable reasons you can choose.

Please, if you feel the need to volunteer and work for the benefit of the world's neediest peoples, I ask this of you. Choose carefully a 'good' charity that you truly identify with, take the time and go to the trouble of finding out the commercial infrastructure of this charity, and also find out exactly what is being accomplished out in the field.

Are there petty and unrelated rules and regulations to follow, especially rules that seem to have little to do with the work in general? Do you have to abide by the charity's religious affiliations when you work with the recipients of your good deeds? Are there conditions of helping that you don't fully understand or totally approve of?

I am strongly suggesting to you, please do your good deeds with a clear understanding of why you need to do them, and how you can effectively bring balance to the bigger picture in any situation that you are helping with.

Working out what charity to support or what good deed you want to do can be an enlightening exercise for anyone to go through, as long as they work out honestly why they want or need to do it. This is important; it is more important than you realise because working through these questions brings into the equation and encompasses deeper Spiritual Truths than you may currently understand. For example, what is more empowering for the hungry child?

1. A meal three times a week sent by donors like you?
2. Sending unconditional Love across the entire continent?

Which of these two choices do you feel is the better choice? There is no right answer to this. I strongly suggest you do both. You help a child to survive in the physical sense, yet at the same time, you empower his or her Spirit in the most magnificent way. And this given help is not selective because you strengthen the band of Hope, Light, and Love around the world, thus bringing the empowerment not just to one hungry child, but to all children, past, present, and future.

Now that seems like a good thing to do, does it not? You help others and at the same time you are joining with the

Light Workers of the World in a communal and collective uplifting of mankind's total empowerment. Not such a bad start for any day.

This is the end of today's session, sweet daughter. Remain joyful; good tidings come to those who expect them and have their heart's door open to receive these blessings.

*The next session began as though the next breath had just been taken.*

I say to you, most beloved reader, be aware of what you give to yourself, as well as any hungry child. As you empower the inner you, you automatically empower all others within your energetic radius. Behind the simple words being written here is the reminder to feed the goose that lays the golden eggs. Get that simile? If you let the goose weaken or die from malnourishment of mind, body, and spirit, the hungry child will not receive any help from you. You will have nothing to give and, even more distressing, you will need to draw energy from others if you are to survive.

I repeat, look after yourself before you jump into saving the hearts, minds, and souls of others. This is not being selfish, and there is a vast difference between being selfish and being nurturing. Being selfish means taking from others to fulfil your own personal wants, and note here that I said 'wants' and not 'needs'. 'Needs' brings in a whole different ballgame, a game that when played well, removes the 'wants' from your life! This self-nurturing is being practical and effective in all ways.

Think of a mother, father, or family member who expends energy driving children all over the country, to sports practise, music, or dance lessons, running here and running there without leaving enough time for eating a relaxing meal or having a decent sleep. And this activity can be non-stop, continuing for days, weeks, or months at a time.

Everyone knows primary carers who do this, and you may even be guilty of this sort of bustling action yourself. Who will this mother, father, or family member be able to help when their energy becomes so depleted that the effectiveness of everything they try and do weakens?

They don't help either themselves or the children. A strong, healthy carer is one who can think clearly, sleep well, organise things to run smoothly, and be balanced enough to be a more effective, supportive parent at all times.

You probably have been taught this saying during child-hood, and it is one that has been taught generally across all societies:

'Do unto others as you would have them do to unto you'.

The words may not be in the same order, but the essential meaning remains. This is a true teaching, but you do need to remember that there is no separation in the truest sense between 'you' and 'others'. All is one, and that is a Universal fact.

Look closely at the words; closely, I said. Begin your charity work in your own home and by doing this, you will bolster the empowerment of all others around you.

Now, I speak here of true personal charity, the good charity of no expectations, of giving freely from the heart and in a way that empowers and enriches both you and all others. Please remember that the 'good' I am talking about is not quite the same 'good' you feel by obediently following religious dogma, or believing that an angry and revengeful Creator is judging your actions to be either good or bad.

A wonderful and godly way is living and giving in a very loving and spiritual manner; this is the only way you can strengthen the hearts of both yourself and the recipient. This action may not always be easy, because you need to intuitively work out exactly what you need to do, what you need to understand, and what you need to let go of or not worry about at the time. While doing all this, at the same time you need to understand truly and honestly what the recipient needs on a deep inner level.

If you ask the right questions, you will get the right answers despite any possible physical distance between you and the recipient of your generosity. I am stressing this point a little. But it is an important point and needs to be addressed.

We [Spirit] are suggesting ways for you to join with the Light Workers of the World in small practical and easily managed steps. This is one such step.

The giving of unconditional love is not charity as such; it is being as true as possible to your personal essence as you consciously connect with your Inner Matrix. And this true connection enriches the understanding of unconditional giving and receiving in any scenario.

Here is a practical exercise for you to try. The next time you volunteer to help in any local event, before you begin the given tasks, ask yourself the following questions and note down the answers that pop into your mind:

Why am I doing this?

By doing this charity work, how does this empower me?

Is there something else that I would rather be doing?

Who gets the benefit of my help? Is this help going to be in their best interest?

Are some of the other volunteers on an ego trip and just using the event to bolster their ego?

If this is so, how do I need to react to their actions?

Is the help and donated items going where they're advertised to be going?

Have I neglected an important need of mine to go to this event?

Do I feel guilty because I truly don't want to be involved at this event?

Do I fully trust my reason for helping? Are these reasons my own or was I steamrolled by a forceful or manipulative person to do this work?

And so on, and so on.

You will likely come up with any number of reasons and questions for yourself. Come up with the questions you need to ask, be honest, be truthful, and be aware. Don't let peer pressure override any of your feelings.

'Charity begins at home' is a true enough adage and goes to a deeper level than you think it may mean.

Where is HOME?

HOME IS YOUR HEART CONNECTION WITH THE CREATIVE INNER UNIVERSAL GOD. THAT IS WHERE YOUR HOME IS.

# 12

# RAINBOW BRIDGES

B y 8 a.m., I was up early and organised, ready and waiting for book dictation to begin, but Samuel's energy was not as strong as usual. I kept getting the advice to wait, to wait. So, I got up from the table and shut the nearby window because a rain shower had begun and was blowing mist into the room and onto the furniture.

This was a welcome distraction. Just to see the rain fall was enjoyable because this district was in the grip of a very dry spell, and the area had just been declared as being in a critical condition and officially recognised as a drought zone. Large areas of Eastern Australia were experiencing drought.

No book dictation was done this morning, but I enjoyed watching the rain falling.

In the following days the weather was humid, hot, and uncomfortable, and there was a cyclone watch in effect. And while musing about previous world news that personally affected me, I was drawn to remember the space shuttle Columbia that disintegrated with the loss of seven astronauts. Earthquakes, floods, fires, and famines had also made global headlines.

Four days later, it was time to resume book dictation.

Good day, dearest daughter. Before we begin work on the manuscript, extra words are appropriate now. The world calamities that you have partially listed above are tangible proof that I speak the truth. There is a quickening, a general world shakeup going on, and this will continue.

The earlier shuttle disintegration you recalled was no random disaster without any upside to it as the press would have you believe, so look to the bigger and ongoing picture here, and you can see how it was a significant gesture that brought a strength of togetherness into the populace.

This is not a cold-hearted statement. Think of it like this; the world population, en-masse, was made aware of the majesty of the human Spirit. It is not only the failure of unsound nuts and bolts or rubber washers that was talked about, but also the coming together of the many citizens around the planet who acknowledged the shining Spirit of the crew.

Lost in space? Never! And note well there is no plural in the way I say 'Spirit of the crew'. There is no separation. No one person is in one spot and another person elsewhere. The disaster was a tangible connector that brought together the World's peoples.

*Samuel, this is not exactly true, this statement about bringing people together. The fundamentalists claimed that the shuttle disaster was a visible sign of the Creator's anger and punishment against America because of that county's 'aggressive retaliation and threats' against terrorists. It seemed to be a dividing event, not a uniting one.*

Wrong, dearest daughter, wrong. The fundamentalists are just a tip of the iceberg. The loudest and most vocal ones do not damage the global reputation of any country. The sign 'proved' the fundamentalists theory is a pseudo-political and fundamental religious sign that is invalid. The shuttle disaster was a global sign, but in a more specific way it was an immediate sign for the Western peoples, each and every one of them. The sign was easy to read: it said to unite in the Strength of Spirit; do not unite behind the leadership of any one man. The sign pointed to a joining of peoples, and not that of separation.

*All this is a bit confusing, Samuel. I feel I can understand what you are saying, but I also feel that many people will never look at the situation from this controversial or unusual point of view. I understand this is a 'big picture' explanation.*

Very well, I will be more direct. The fundamentalists of any religious persuasion shoot themselves in the foot when they contend that the Columbia disaster was a sign from the God of their choice, a sign that pointed the finger of blame at nations for whatever reason, and that this specific disaster proved beyond doubt that the fundamentalists of all persuasions have the only truthful creed.

You see, aggression comes in many forms, both small and large. Deprivation of liberties, nonsensical and vicious religious rulings, even inane rites and intolerances are on a par with the direst aggression. How do you measure one aggression against another? With a measuring stick that has marks along one side?

The saying 'The pot calling the kettle black' is applicable here, because both the kettle and the pot have been blackened over the fire. The Columbia explosion was a wakeup call to all sides to rejoice in spiritual togetherness, and not of separation. Therefore, I say to all who read these words, the tragedy was indeed a godly gesture, but you all need to be very aware about how you personally interpreted this gesture.

Indeed, you don't really need to interpret it at all; you need to intuitively understand it. And if this is done well, with integrity and honesty, you will see this event from an entirely different angle. Religious fundamentalists, terrorists, and all other strict and rigid creeds will try and enforce an official belief that is of either an aggressive or victimisation nature. My words in this book have repeatedly suggested that you have to do your own thinking. Do not believe blindly everything you hear and see.

The shuttle 'disaster' proved to be a catalyst of a kind, not because it was so different from other tragedies such as floods, fires, and famines, but because the images were captured on worldwide media platforms. And most of the global population have seen these images in one way or another.

It is a unifying event, a unification of the Spirit of Humanity.

What eventuates from this is still in flux. There is urgency in our words to you. Please, think about the world news and events of importance for yourself, because as I have repeatedly suggested, most of the modern-day leaderships in power have hidden agendas that are not compatible with mankind's empowerment and ultimate survival. Do you:

Trust a political leader because he or she goes to church or a place of worship weekly?

Trust a despot because he says repeatedly that he is good?

Trust a liar to tell the truth because he says he is telling the truth?

Please, do yourself and all others the favour of working out your own opinions.

Connect into the true globally active blanket of Love and Light that you now know exists. It is there under your nose, in, above, and below your nose. Don't be lazy and allow others to do the thinking for you. Do your own thinking.

More global signs will be 'sent' from All That Is, the Creator or Deity of your choice, and it is up to each individual to deeply understand the bigger picture that is being shown each time an event of attention getting power is unleashed. The power resides in you, whether you are resting at home, working in the fields, or sailing the seven seas.

Question orders. Question laws and restrictions. Please know that within your heart you will need to understand why each and every global event occurs as they do, and especially remember to think deeply about the 'big picture' reasons. The true reasons why, when, and how these events occurred will be seen as signposts for humankind to follow, and as signs that show the path to Home.

This is the dilemma for you all at the moment. It is easy to go along with the official rules, regulations, and explanations, but to make it easier for you to survive as you are majestically meant to survive you need to step into your own power of decision making. To do or not to do, that is the question each person will need to answer, and answer quickly.

For now, the shuttle Columbia disaster will still be used as our example for the following insights and suggestions. Let us see the positive, or significant, side of this event and note how it fitted as interlocking pieces in the proverbial jigsaw you call Life.

*Well, that was interesting, but I reckon Samuel was just lightly touching on the subject, sort of skating on the crest of a deep well of information; there is a lot more that can be said, but this was the end of dictation for the day.*

*When the next session began there had been lovely, gentle rain falling, and even now as I write there are big beads of moisture hanging determinedly from the clothesline. They are like little rainbows shining in the weak sunlight. You can almost feel the trees on the hillside relaxing, and their stress levels dropping. The drought has been broken at last.*

Good day, dearest daughter. Indeed, each drop of rain is a whole Universe in itself. The rainbows are symbolic bridges of light between your personal Universe and all others. Let us continue this chapter about bridges.

In a significant way, the shuttle disaster was a globally watched bridging event; it was an event flaring across the sky for all to see and try to understand. Bridges link between two or more points; in fact, they link between multiple points, and they link and span spaces in multiple ways.

*According to the Wordsworth Concise English Dictionary, "bridge" means among other structures giving access across, i.e., a river, a road. A place to see from, i.e. a ship captain's bridge, i.e., a piece of wood to give violin strings support. Anything that connects to both sides, across a gap. To connect the extremities of.*

Say the word 'bridge' again with different emotions and in a multiple of ways. However you say it, it will always suggest a link and connector to multiple factors, so do you still think the space shuttle Columbia falling from the sky sent out the exact same message to everyone? Of course not; this point has already been raised. The event had a similar message for all, but this message was shown in different forms, strengths, and areas as needed, and not just in a blanket of singular meaning.

Let me expound on this a little more. At any specific time, a person will only receive the messages that they are capable of receiving and understanding at that specific time in their life.

Therefore, the Columbia message was received by each person in a general way, and also in a very individualistic and personal manner. It was not as a blanket 'like it or lump it' type of ultimatum. Each person dreamt a different dream about this event, and their reactions in these dreams were very different and individualistic from that of all other dreamers.

Yet the dreamer needs to remember and understand why they dreamt as they did. Here I speak briefly of dreaming, because everyone on your beautiful Earth will have had dreams that link them with the message substance of this godly gesture. Even the natives in the densest jungle who have not heard of this event through any media outlet will have dreamt about it, because everyone will have been connected via the dream bridges.

Each and every person alive has dreamt, will dream, or went on a dream journey into the dreaming realm where the event made sense, and where it was shown to each soul how it fitted into the bigger picture. All you have to do is to remember your dreams and you will have the answers to everything.

*There was a strong sense of fun and humour coming through as Samuel dictated these words about remembering dreams.*

The bridge of dreams is a powerful and rock-solid conduit for carrying unlimited amounts of insightful information into the everyone's heart. Trust this bridge because it is one that never fails.

Even if you cannot remember your dreams about this event, do not panic and run around in an agitated frenzy. The Inner You has received and stored all you need to know, and it is now the turn of the consciously aware 'you' to make the effort to be quiet and still, and effectively meditate so you can access this data.

Please remember that meditation is only one way for this information to come out into the light of day. Even if the information is unknown on a conscious level, your actions, thoughts, and beliefs will still be affected by whatever insights can sneak into your thoughts via the cracks in your mind's busy daily schedule.

Look and see if you can do something a little differently than you usually do it, or see if you can become spontaneously more reflective and catch brief moments of introspection at random times during the day. You may read a newspaper article and see a different slant to what seems to be a straightforward statement. You may look at a neighbour with a little more curiosity and wonder what they are thinking about, and how they are reacting to the global news. You may note yourself doing many little things that you don't normally do.

This is the effect of the Inner Knowing at work. It may be wispy and sneaky and difficult to grasp, but it is determined to allow needed knowledge and insights to become known. Be aware of impulses to express this inner knowledge when the tendrils come drifting through the cracks. Allow the dream bridge to expand and flow into your intuitive expressiveness. Allow the insights to flow unhindered over these connecting rainbow bridges of Light. Allow yourself permission to understand whatever your Deepest Soul is trying to tell you about your connection to any significant gesture.

If you have read and understood what has been written thus far, you will know you are intrinsically involved and connected on all levels with what happened with the shuttle. This is fact, not fiction.

Now that you have understood this, look again at the so-called terrorists, the angry and the violent people who are active in your world at this time. They also, each and every one of them, have been given the same data, the same general understandings that you have been given, sometimes through their dreaming states or through other means of communication, yet they refuse to understand it for what it is. Or they understand it, but they choose to deliberately not acknowledge its existence.

For most of them the data is still in their dream storage, and it is their personal choice whether they access it or not. Despite all the determined, sneaky efforts of their inner resources, there may have been little chance for this inner knowing to creep through the cracks of hatred and fanaticism into the conscious mind.

Again, all people are joined together in their dreaming, and all people have been shown the message of this event. It is up to each individual to allow this message to manifest into the Light.

The bridge is always there, always open, and always understanding, but it is up to you, a person of immense willpower, to put the first step into action and walk freely across this connecting bridge. Let the controlling willpower have a holiday, but it may strongly resist being shunted aside, so be firm, send it away, and allow your heart to lead you into God's Light. Dreams and the inner dreamscapes have been purposely made to accommodate this type of informational access.

What did you do when you remembered your dream connection to the shuttle event? Did you absentmindedly immediately forget about it, or did you think that it was a curious or interesting dream, and then forgot about it? Did you go into great analytical discussions with friends on the more obscure meanings of the dream? What exactly did you do?

You probably needed to start by accepting the dream as a valid message for you. Note well how you acted, what you saw, heard, and felt in your dream. Just accept it. For the ones who were shown something to do, if possible, just do it without reservation.

For the majority, the dream message may be a jumble of unconnected images that are difficult to understand. Some may remember terror, panic, or being frightened about something. It doesn't matter what you dreamt, just remember it and say to yourself that yes, indeed, this is a message meant for me, and when it is timely to do so, I will remember it, I will understand it, and I will know what to do. Give yourself permission to open up to this message when you need to.

See, that wasn't hard, was it? The Inner You will do what is needed at the time, as long as the control has been eased.

It's all very well, you may say, but what is the point of everyone in the world connecting on a dream level if the bad guys ignore the messages or refuse to understand what they saw in their dream messages? This question is not a valid one.

The bad guys come in many shapes and sizes, and from a multitude of cultural and ethnic backgrounds, but despite their blinkered state, the knowledge of dream messages is within their matrix and cannot be deleted.

As more and more Workers of the Light remember their dreams and implement actions of empowerment, the tightly held focus or control of the bad guys gets bombarded with battery rams of the Light. The bad guys may not consciously sense this happening because their focus is elsewhere, but as more Light Warriors strengthen the Blanket of Love around the Earth, the more the Light can accomplish in creating cracks in the controlling dogma, hatred, and ignorance.

The intensity of the Light increases and when this intensity reaches a certain level, the Light will burst forth and it will emerge from the most tightly clamped down places; it will shine forth in all Glory and Love, and it will be unstoppable. Therefore, do not despair of the bad guys winning. You are as much in control of your world as they think they are in control of their world. Relax, release, and rejoice because you hold the trump card.

Relax, release, and rejoice!

This is the message from me to you.

*It was seven days since the last book dictation, a week where my attention was on family concerns that needed to be dealt with. A gentle rain had been falling on and off during this time, the trees and grasses were greening, and the world looked fresh and clean. I don't mean to be giving weather news, but I was enjoying the newness and freshness around me. All the little creatures that shared their living spaces in the local area with me had been doing the same.*

I am here and ready to roll!

*There was such a wonderful feeling of fun and happiness emanating from the personality 'focus' of energy I know as Samuel, as he entered my space. He brought such vibrancy and good humour with him, and it was a pleasure to welcome him each time.*

You see, bridges are rainbows. They are hopes, they are friendships, they are family, and they are everything. Do you honestly think you are alone, or lonely? If you do feel like this, you are allowing an illusion of your own making to come into being and to distort your true perceptions.

Just for a moment imagine yourself standing in a meadow, a peaceful open field somewhere. Imagine you are standing alone, yet in truth you are being helped to stand upright by unlimited bands of energy. You are being fully supported by energy bridges. You are intrinsically a part of everything, and the scaffolding frameworks of everything are these rainbow bridges.

From our side of the dividing veil, you are a brightly illuminated circle of Light surrounded by further flares of flashing Light. Quite a beautiful sight, indeed, and a sight you would be thrilled and awed to see for yourself. What Light! What Love! What beauty! What patterns!

To see you, and you, and you in your truest form lifts the heartstrings, tugs at the emotions, and connects the onlooker to the Creator with an even deeper measure of Love and Light, and with the absolute feeling of being at Home.

Oh, what glorious sights are Souls and their bridges to the pasts, the presents, and the futures! Do you feel I wax too lyrical for a personality described in the biblical passages as a stern and judgemental individual? Well, I ask this of you: Consider who gets annoyed when they are awoken from a deep, deep resting. Do you?

*I think this may have been in reference to the biblical story when Samuel was brought back from the 'dead' to act as a conduit between God and the populace, to also give advice and judgement in matters of concern. The Old Testament: The Book of Samuel 28. 14–16.*

*If this is so, it was very much a tongue in cheek remark. The story may or may not be accurate, but we all know someone who has been annoyed at being woken from a deep sleep at one time or another.*

No one can describe in mere words what a soul looks like. It is impossible to put into words or to give an accurate description of the true nature of a soul in any language.

The act of trying to describe a sliver of God—that is, you in your Light form—undermines to a certain degree the integral connection needed to see this Light. This is because 'trying' is a doing word, a stressful word, a word that implies that there is never going to be a successful outcome to what is being attempted.

The only way I can truly describe the soul is not to try, so this is an interesting conundrum for writers! Even talking about the 'bridges' as we have done so briefly does not do justice to the concept of the sheer magnificent weblike connections and light patterns that are the framework of the universe around you. Nor is it easy to accurately describe you in a more personal way as the all-seeing, all-knowing Eternal, Infinite, and Universal Soul that you are.

How can I adequately describe to you how I see the bridges that span across time zones, and across the ancient pasts and into the ancient futures? How can I explain the glowing, pulsating Cord of Light that quivers, stretches, condenses, and thrives, between you and all else in Creation? The mind boggles, doesn't it?

Your personal bridges make a web of Light that is Creation, and that is the Universe. It is a pulsing, glowing web of dreams, bridges, hopes, hatred, love, endurance, and curiosity. A most magnificent, magnificent web! Now that I have brought forth this image of the totality of the web of Light Bridges that you are the centre of, you may note something else at this time.

Yes, the computer communication links of the World Wide Web. This is a perfect physical world analogy of what I say. Just remember that I speak in general terms of a much higher vibrational Web of Light; the reality-based computer web is of a network thriving in a coarser and denser vibrational energy. You cannot see your electronic messages whizzing around the world, yet you know they travel along set lines.

My Web of Light is ever more flexible, not always seen, and is even more powerful and always in movement. Yes, the descriptive name of the World Wide Web is an excellent one. The World is crisscrossed with untold electronic webbing, so just imagine this webbing, then go that next step further and see yourself moving amongst your own moving, undulating Web of Life.

A beautiful picture, isn't it?

*That is a beautiful image, Samuel. In Native and Shamanic cultures, the Spider represents the weaving of the Web of Life, a crisscrossing of strands and multiple pathways making a web either large or small, and multidimensional.*

The interesting and more immediate of these 'bridges' are the ones that are in your focal range right now. You have different 'bridges' to use when the main Soul of You is experiencing different dimensions. The real 'you' is the main energy matrix that manipulates the physical body while it exists in this dimension. The actual physical person you know as 'you' is only a splinter of the main Soul of You.

Your Main Soul has energy gestalts flowing out into multiple realms, and these usually remain unknown to you from the standpoint of your present circumstances. These flowing filaments are like questing beams of Light, fully aware, and fully experiencing whatever the Main Soul needs these adventurous parts of Itself to experience.

This Core Soul of You has unlimited numbers of these filaments thrusting out and bridging out over time and space. You are a Spark of this Core Soul, and this Core Soul is a spark of another Core Soul, ad infinitum. They are all Creator Energy. Do you begin to see the vast connections you have? YOU ARE A BRIDGE TO EVERYTHING IN EXIS-TENCE AND ALL THAT HAS BEEN AND EVER WILL BE. The Web of Life does not work on one level only as does the electronic web. Your Web of Life never stops, and it has no boundaries it must stay within. It flows through layer after layer of realties, in all the different Realms and Universes in creation.

How can mere words speak truly of this magnificence? How can mere words describe to you how magnificent and godly you are? How can mere words begin to describe your potential, your strengths, your knowledge, and your vibrational force of Love?

Are you beginning to see what I see? Do you see the Light of the Light that you are created from, glowing within your heart? How can you not get up from your chair, raise your arms into the air in celebration, and shout:

"I will make a difference! I will bring peace and love to all things! I am Love and Light! I will change my world for the better!"

How can you not do this? The power of one is immense; the power of two is even more immense and intense; the power of multitudes lights up the Universe.

Do you want a bridge to peace and serenity that spans your world? It is there, already in place; all you have to do is walk over it.

*I loved the beautiful imagery, and as Samuel wrote the words, I got visions and flashes of what he was describing. I realised these flashes were the tiniest glimpses of a universe or universes that he talked about, and I still find it hard to comprehend the immensity of it all, but these fractional visions were almost overwhelming in the emotional intensity they brought to my heart.*

*The words were coming so powerfully, it was almost as though Samuel was on a high mountain top and shouting out the words for all peoples on the planet to hear.*

You feel so, dearest daughter? Imagery is illusion; the bridges I speak about are real in all ways. At times, your illusions stop you from seeing what your true self and heritage is.

*A sense of humour makes unpalatable truths easier to hear, so I was glad Samuel smile das these words were spoken.*

Well, why should I not smile? I see beauty, strength, and love in all people; the bridges to empowerment, peace, and harmony in your world are not too deeply hidden. The Light Workers, and the ones who march for hope and peace, are now stirring up some sludge, and when this transmuted sludge resettles or disperses, a new world view will appear.

Analogies are a way to show how events may happen in any given time frame and/or probable futures. In their own way, the analogies have validity in reality simply because the illusion has been activated. Imagery and illusions are potent triggers for change.

Believe in the power of each individual to bring forth the change that will, when combined en-masse, take a balanced step towards mankind's evolution and transcendence into the true Godly heritage.

This is the end of this chapter, dearest daughter. The next chapter will be about the effects of bridge building. Go about your daily activities with love. You have an interesting time ahead of you.

# 13

# JUMPING BOOKS

We can see the day when people begin to understand the deep connection to the God of their Creation. This connection is not one where a servant needs to do certain things in specific ways to keep their Lord and Master happy, but one with a loving and all-encompassing connection as one has to a brother, sister, family, or self.

A few among the many now see, or eventually will see, this concept and connection as the absolute truth, and will accept unconditionally the knowledge that they are a vital part of the Whole. For others, it is not always easy to understand because of the belief that they are powerless to alter anything in the bigger scheme of things.

These others are the people who have not yet begun to understand that they are able to create their own realities, that they can become even more effective and successful as a human personality experiencing creativity in the physical levels. Forget the vast amount of curious literature that suggests humankind were slaves of another species, or that there is no hope for salvation from all unpleasant situations unless the masses, 'Do as they are told to do.'

The way to 'salvation' is quite simple: You need to remember who you are.

You need to shake off the blindfolds of restrictive religious, cultural, social practices, and teachings. You need to have the courage to step out of the darkness and into the arena where the Light shines brightly and illuminates everything about you. Because it is only then that you can intuitively and clearly see where you are standing.

You will see with eyes that understand this 'where'. You will know and connect strongly with like-minded people who stand in this brightly lit area beside you. Oh, dearest people, you will 'see' as though for the first time, a true picture of who, what, why, and where you are, who you have been and will be.

You will see how you have accepted and dealt with numerous and varied challenges and experiences. You will 'see' how to clearly 'see'.

> So now you see the big green sea
>
> You quietly watch and let it be
>
> To ripple and roil, and to shiver and shake
>
> The sea is to see, the Creator to make
>
> You see, you see, you see?

There, that is a little fun ditty!
*There was such a good feeling of fun and light heartedness in the room.*

It is not exactly classical poetry, is it, but it's not too bad for a three second time limit!

The issue being discussed is not difficult to understand. You are all being given multiple chances to remember who you really are. You are being encouraged by God, Great Spirit, All That Is, the Creator—take your pick—to put up your hand and acknowledge not only who you truly are, but to understand how you have the innate ability to make a major and enlightened difference to your planet, to your Universe, whenever, whatever, or wherever the situation is you find yourself in.

You can help bring peace and plenty in a practical way to the Earth and all her denizens. You can be an effective and pivotal piece of the environmental, global, and cosmological jigsaw puzzle.

The original essay that started the whole communication with my dearest daughter and is recorded in the Introduction, suggested that there is much confusion about what questions people need to ask, especially in stressful times and when they are in panic mode. Who will be there to show the people the answers to these unasked questions?

As the years roll by, you will see more and more Light Workers—Warriors of Light—appearing amongst you; many will emerge from the most unlikely of places. They are, and will be, stepping out of the shadows and placing themselves squarely into the Light where everybody can see them and the actions they take, and where everyone is able to listen to the teachings that come from the Source.

Emerging into the public notice takes not only great courage of the heart, but an unconditional and total Love of all things. These people have remembered who they truly are and will be trying to help everyone else remember who they truly are. As you know, when you stand high over a crowd you can see further, but at the same time you put yourself out in the open as a target, a target that will be challenged vigorously by any of the prejudiced and blinkered ones who wish to be aggressive.

The original essay ended by saying that there is hope. Never forget that. There is more hope being publicly displayed in your world right now than you may realise. There is hope and help from all the Gods. When you think about this, it is not a bad backstop to have on a stressful and unrestful day.

I have already spoken about these Light Warriors, the stout hearted and enlightened people who can be found amongst you, these magnificent souls who stand up strongly for what they believe, and do so despite the possible danger to them-selves. I have also spoken about the Blanket of Love these special people work to strengthen and expand.

I have not yet spoken very much about the busy Spirit Helpers who are effective Bearers of the Light. You have your human heroes and heroines who you look up to for leader-ship, and you also have Teachers and Leaders from the realm of Spirit who you can look to for great advice and leadership.

I am not talking generally about religious leaders, who reside in the physical reality, and I do acknowledge there are some very effective ones working in the public arena. Rather, I am talking about the unseen Spirit Teachers and Helpers. Just because they do not appear on your television screen does not mean they don't exist.

Now, how do I simplify this vast and unlimited subject?

*I got the giggles at this question. I never thought that Samuel would ever pause to consider what words needed to be used, because the insights, informational patterns, and words all seemed to flow so effortlessly each time the book dictation was in session.*

Oh, I see my pen-wielding friend is having a jest with me because I wrote the above words. Well, dear one, it is not a pause of time I act upon but a pause of logic. How do I write, in a few words, logical and reasoned prose about a subject that many perceive to be illogical? The subject of Spirit Guides and Guardian Angels has been written about and talked about ad infinitum since time began and it will continue to be thus.

No, I try to correlate what needs to be said with what is being said. To note the sheer volume of written works on, for example, Angelic personalities, is to see a mountain range of wriggling, contorting, and exuberant words, words that sometimes make sense and many times do not. If I can see this confusion from my vantage point, then how may a mere mortal work out what words speak the truth and what words are untruthful?

*Again, there were great smiles as well as gentle and teasing humour flooding the room. I think Samuel was challenging us to shout out in defiance, "Hey! I'm not a mere mortal! I am a Universal, Eternal, Infinite, and Immortal Soul!"*

Hey there, dear readers, it is a minefield out there! You know you have to follow your gut instinct at all times… and that means following your intuition for those of you with short memories.

Step warily between the dancing words in the multitude of books until you are intuitively drawn towards a collection of them. A minefield of untruthful words is a difficult thing to wend your way safely through, especially if there have been decoys of truthful words hidden here and there amongst the deceptive ones.

So, how do you move through all the literature that has been and will be offered for your consideration on the subject of spirit, enlightenment, and godly deeds? Keep in mind that I include this book you are reading now, amongst these many.

*There was such good humour and a tangible physical feeling that a strong, fun bubble formed around the desk while this section was being dictated.*

How do you know which Angels to call upon for help and advice when you find yourself in a situation that needs this extra help? How do you know which Spirit Guide to call upon to help you to safely navigate through the minefield of words? There are many, many angels and spirit guides—you know this because it has already been written about in elaborate and concise detail—with each angel and guide possessing specialist skills or expertise in specific fields of endeavour.

How do you find your own personal angel or guide to lead you, to advise you and help and comfort you?

A point here, I placed the word 'lead' in the sentence for a valid reason. Briefly, you will never find an angel, guide [et al] to lead you anywhere, and you will never be forced or ordered to blindly follow any directives given. You will, however, be shown and then invited to take a certain path, or invited to follow any offered advice, for example, to select, then read a certain book. See the difference?

When you ask for spiritual advice, Helpers from the Realm of Spirit will be only too willing to assist and advise, or encourage you to choose from various options they may be able to bring to your attention. You don't need to know the names of the angels or helpers; you don't need to know what they look like or which ones specialise in helping people to choose the correct texts and book to read. All you need to know is this:

Know these Angels are nearby and ready to help you.

Know that all you need to do is give them permission to help you.

And when this is done, and this permission is forthcoming, hey presto! A little sneaky piece of gut instinct breaks out of the deep, dark inner dungeon; comes bounding up the stairway; and you will then be able to hear a whispering in your ear about what book you need to read at any given time. You will be drawn towards the texts that contain some truths and relevant information, especially truths that help you to understand and resolve whatever situation you are dealing with.

Just call on your Inner God for the answer to any which, what, where, or when question, and a Godly Messenger will be in contact with you. Sometimes the questioner is open enough to feel, hear, or see these messengers and so a distinct and more detailed partnership is born.

Even so, the 'whole' messenger is not usually visible, nor all the words audible to the receiver, and only a small sliver or a portion of the whole may be glimpsed. Therefore, even if the receiver writes truly of what appears to them, there is still a great deal that will not be connected with or put into words.

Think of the iceberg floating in the ocean. The dazzling tip is seen above the waves and the rest is hidden deep within the watery depths. Even a good diver will get to see more of the iceberg, but only a small facet or face of it at the time. Never is the whole iceberg visible at the one time.

If you have been brought up to pray to various saints [or sinners] or other well-known spiritual figures, you probably know by heart the name and attribute of what each particular saint, angel, or helper is good at doing. If you have prayed to a specific saint and asked for a boon of some sort, a boon that the named saint is known to be good at giving, and yet despite all your efforts and despite all entreaties you have not received the guidance that you have asked for, you may have a problem.

You may wonder if you have prayed to the right angel. Maybe another choice would have been better. You start to think that you didn't light enough candles or offer enough food at the altar, say the correct words, or wear the right clothes. The 'what if' scenarios play with your mind, resulting in more doubt and stressful fields of uncertainty enfolding you.

Just ask. Talk with and communicate with your Inner God, and the correct Angel or Helper will be 'contacted'. You may never get to know this Angelic One's name or whether he or she or it has wings, a halo, or a white tunic, or breeches. It doesn't matter! If you are able to intuit a name, you are being given a handle to hold, so use it.

*A delightful sense of fun was still drifting, floating, swirling, and dancing all over the room.*

If you are not given a name, don't bust your boiler with indignation and stress because you feel you are not deemed important enough to be properly introduced. Go with the flow; just let go of all control and relax. You can add this saying to the massive pile of adages you already have heard.

*Huge smiles were everywhere and there was such a strong feeling of irreverent fun spiralling with amusement around the words, because maybe it is a subject people take too seriously, when Samuel feels there is no need for it to be serious.*

If your intuition says everything is alright, then accept whoever and whatever comes to advise you and lead you through the minefield of texts.

The hardest thing for you to do is to trust enough of the inner processes to let the emotional and conscious controls relax, and become open fully to the incoming information. Then allow what is the most important step in this process: giving yourself permission to accept this help.

This is actually quite a difficult action for many to do because they equate it to a loss of personal control, and this is a pity, because not allowing or giving permission to accept help implies the conscious control of your stubborn willpower remains intact. However, you can control and order the willpower to disappear for a while, and it will do so, because you are the boss of 'you'.

*Again, there was a lot of good humour about. Samuel seemed to be having a lot of fun with this subject.*

Therefore, here are some suggestions on how to work out which words or teachings you will find helpful to read at the right time.

Invite the God of You to suggest a text, book to read, etc. Give permission for this advice to be lovingly received by you. Believe fully that you will be given the right advice. Trust the messenger and the advice given, in any of the many ways it may come to you. Trust what you intuit, even if you do not immediately understand the message.

Know that you will always be given what you need, and not necessarily what you think you want.

Don't wait for a book to fall from a shelf and hit you on your head. Open up to your intuition and scan the bookshelves. Do something physical to kickstart the search.

If a book does fall from a shelf and hit you on the head, know that an Angel, Guide, or Helper pushed it and you are meant to read it. If it falls at your feet, pick it up because it will have some sort of insight or clue on what path you need to take.

Thank the Angel for hitting you on the head with the book.

Get the idea?

We finish for the morning, dearest daughter.

*This was definitely a fun session. The good humour and laugh-ter seemed to be bubbling along with the words. I really enjoyed the whole experience, and the imagery that came flooding in was such fun.*

If you already have a working relationship with a Guard-ian Angel, by all means continue to work with this Beloved One; just go that one step deeper into an even more empower-ing relationship. Become as a brother or sister to this beautiful One; don't stay on the level of a follower, following meekly behind the leader. Become a participant in an effective and active partnership by working together in whatever way you can. Now, if you have this kind of relationship already in place and working well, that is great and I sincerely mean that.

But have you had an in-depth chat lately with your angelic partner on what up-to-date advice you need about your ongo-ing spiritual quest? Or has the chatting been more of an every-day pastime, such as discussions about your daily list of the mundane and banal sort of things? For example, where do you find the money to pay the latest phone bill, or how can you get a better car, or find a new dog trainer to help with the control of your dog's loud barking? Are you utilising your angelic part-nership to its full potential? I thought not.

It is not always easy being human and keeping well bal-anced, with one foot on the ground and the other bridging into the world of Spirit. A straddling across any boundary into two very different areas often brings unbalance and uncertainty, or at the very least, a concentration of focus on one side more so than on the other.

It is in this type of situation that you need to have created a solid bridge between both places: a bridge that is stable, bal-anced, and flexible enough for your focus to be able to flick back and forth instantly and without impediment, and most importantly, without the threat of you toppling off the span.

However, it is easy to be human and to be a full partner in your spiritual relationships. Ask for advice on how to walk the minefield of metaphysical and religious literature. Out there, in a pile of books and on a shelf somewhere, is a book you need to read. It will be a book that will have an answer for you, or an insight that points you along the path of enlightened learning. A book with words of wisdom that you need to read and understand. Maybe it is not even the words within the book that you need to read; it well may be that in the act of finding this book you are being guided to, you meet a person who you find out later is in fact the messenger.

So, dear readers, be aware of what you watch, see, or hear from your entertainment and educational sources. Ask for guidance from your Creator at all times, so that you have a sporting chance of finding what you need to read or understand.

The truth for you is out there and you need to be able to determine what it is when it hits you on the head. If you cannot find what you are looking for, even after searching diligently with or without any extra help, you may have to sit down with pen and paper and write your own truth.

Everyone can survive and do so successfully; all it takes is a little knowledge on how the various information systems work. For example, if you find that you are perplexed or distressed about the troubles and woes that are afflicting the planetary energy at any time, then simply go to the cosmic Reference Library, or ask your Angel what text, spoken word, or actions can explain these World situations in a way that you can identify with. It is up to you to make the first move to find this information. You have a guide; you have all the resources needed. Go for it!

Dearest daughter, this is where we finish this morning. I bid you a beautiful day.

*There was a lovely sense of fun floating everywhere while this chapter was being dictated. Years ago, I had a series of incidences and coincidences when books actually did fall from the shelves and hit me on the head, so I know this does happen.*

*Another time, a collection of three books fell from a secure place and landed in my arms. Naturally, they contained information that I needed at that time.*

*Another day, I had been sitting at a table when a book seemed to move from a side table several feet from where I was sitting and land with a thump at my feet. Information was being literally thrown at me, and this type of interaction continues to this day.*

*This has occurred with other objects also, i.e., an umbrella, and events such as these continue to happen now and again, sometimes sneakily and sometimes not!*

*Ask around. Talk to your friends about this subject. I bet that someone will have a story about a book falling from the shelf as they stood nearby, or maybe an instance when out of the blue they had been given a book to read, a book that contained the perfect help for them.*

# 14

# ADDICTIONS

This chapter will be about a different insight, and please, don't push this idea away before you read fully what I say and have thought about it. The days of the scattered few and hard to find Teachers of the Truth are long gone, and that suggests that the times have changed, the communication techniques have changed, and many multitudes of Truth Teachers are now emerging from the most unlikely of places.

This makes it easier for anyone to find insightful inspiration when and where they need it. You have also just read about this in my earlier words, so now you can go that one step further and ask your inner guru this: "Am I such a teacher? Am I one of the helpful teachers?"

This question is a valid one and the answer should be evident to you immediately because there is no line of separation between Light Warriors, Truth Teachers and inspirational people. So, yes. Of course, you are. The level of teaching is not in question, it is the application and intent that is important. You only have to remember what you know and then help other people remember what they know. Correct? But also wrong, because there is another layer to this story.

So here is the little twist. You are not only remembering your strengths and true identity, but you are also learning how to deal with the shadow side of learning. What comes through to you in your quest for enlightenment will not always be a ball of loving, shiny, fuzzy, warm knowledge.

As you bring to light your inner memories, you will remember everything: the good and bad, the light and dark, and the balance and lack of balance. Therefore, as you do your spiritual remembering you will have many 'dark' memories to deal with as well as warm and fuzzy ones.

As you now know, these dark memories will put you into 'dark' situations to help you understand and deal with them. You see, everything is a balance and even though you may see the beauty and feel the love of Spirit strongly, you will also see clearly what is going on in the darker areas of your life.

Just to stop you falling over in a panic, I tell you truly the strength of Love makes the heart stronger because it is also the Love of clarity and is most impressive in its strength. As your Inner Core grows in power, balance, and surety, the clearer you can see and the more you will understand the shadow memories.

Please do not put limits on what you want to learn or remember. For instance, don't say to yourself that only 'white light' or good memories of the Universal Knowledge are allowed to be reborn into your conscious awareness. The Inner You knows you cannot divide a whole and still expect to see the total picture.

It will bring forth the memories you may class as dark ones, and some of these could be the residue or buried memories from situations and events from the many past lives you have cycled through over time, lives in which you have struggled to understand the Universal Laws. And it is now a grand time to go over the basics again.

Some of these ancient memories may be buried so deep that, when recalled, you don't feel any connection to them and believe they are nothing to do with you. You feel they are not your memories. But they probably are.

Look around you at this time; look around at the mental health checks and balances of your compatriots. Also look carefully at the younger ones in your society because a group lesson may be emerging and coalescing at this time, and it's like a huge, surging memory recall rumbling into reality, especially amongst these young people.

They are bringing forth their most deeply buried memories because it is time to deal with them, and they have decided en-masse to do this together. It could also be time to deal with their internal spiritual balance, to work through the shadows and emerge into the balanced space of clear thinking and clear seeing of what is eventuating within their personal spaces and global arenas. Do you follow that?

A culture where drug use is rampant is always known as a camouflaged culture. The users are the people who, as a collective group, cannot bear to face the opening up of their memories; they are unwillingly to recall what it is they know they need to recall. They live with a seesawing of their emotions. And by the way, I class drug use rather widely and see it as the continued use of anything that is addictive, be it chemical substances, food, alcohol, activities, and so on.

Do you think this description of mine is a simplistic view of what society in general sees as a huge, huge problem? It is not, because all users show a lack of confidence in themselves, and they have a strong but groundless fear of the unknown.

Remove this lack, this fear, and the need for camouflaging addictions will fly out the window.

*That's a controversial statement, Samuel.*

Maybe, but who among you will ever be able to prove it wrong?

*Great humour came along with these words, but it was the gentle sort of quiet, fatherly benevolence, and not the comical guffaws that were so frequent from Samuel.*

This issue of drug usage is coming to a crisis, because so many people are being caught up in these addictive practices and have nowhere to go with this burden on their shoulders. Health workers can offer advice on the physical aspects of behaviour, but for true healing to occur a spiritual flowering from deep within each person needs to be encouraged.

You see, addiction of any kind is an inner problem, and not one that can be released or fixed in an external way. The person with the addiction will eventually recall what they are trying to hide from, despite their frantic efforts to keep this information deeply hidden.

During sleep, the Inner Soul tries its best to let needed knowledge flow freely; therefore, dreams are an important element to help these people unlock what they don't want to remember. And because this is an active internal dialogue, some dreamers bring forth from the depths the most amazing, terrifying, and daunting situations imaginable that they try to block out at any cost.

However, if you allow these addicted people to work through their fears in a spiritual or non-dogmatic and non-judgemental way, they will regain faith in themselves to withstand any scary or untenable internal knowledge. Their fears will lessen, their inner flower can blossom into full bloom, and their heart sings of its release from the prison of fear. This freedom from fear is exhilarating and is infectious in its joy.

Think this through. With so many people dealing with major and soul destroying addictions, and many more becoming addicted as you read these words, why do you think this increase is happening now?

Simply put, there is a tidal wave of people trying to suppress their inner knowledge, and this wave is pushing against the individual and collective willpower.

This inner knowledge needs to come forth and into the Light, and it will try to break through the suppressive layers wherever possible. Yes, a huge surge of remembering is battering at the 'gates' of many, and in their distress these many are turning to addictions, fear of failure, phobias, and unsocial behaviours.

This wave gathers strength, it gathers momentum, and it only needs a tiny turning of a key, a tiny sliver of insight and understanding to find the chink in the wall that allows the barriers to come tumbling down and to effectively disperse the tidal wave of fear and addiction.

And when this huge wave of knowledge and remembering comes crashing through the barriers and flows into conscious awareness, the need for suppressive addictions will fade away and be replaced by another 'state' of being.

Bear with me for a moment here. Imagine someone who has been in a dark place for a while, then someone else suddenly flashes a bright light in their face. There will be a moment of blindness and confusion for this person, a moment of blindness that will leave as the eyes adjust to the new level of light.

The Light dazzles! The previously addicted ones will be dazzled for a moment or two by the Light, the clarity, and the immensity of what is coming forth, what is coming into view.

There will be a moment of confusion, but this phase does not last very long. And the larger and the more powerful the volume of Light that comes through with these newly released memories and knowledge, the clearer the following thoughts and feelings.

At this stage, the fears and the addictive behaviours rarely return and each person can begin to deal with whatever has emerged from deep within their fears in a direct way, and by doing this introspection, they can become a powerful advocate for enlightened change. This emanation of enlightened change ripples out, ripples out into the community.

Are you beginning to see some sense in the timing of this 'wave'? It is at this time in mankind's collective evolution that a tidal wave of insightful people is needed to become effective teachers and leaders. Talk about a marvellous backup plan!

All that is needed to trigger this reaction is a small golden key that opens up the smallest chink in the armour of all those who fear. Help them find this key by allowing your Light to shine so strongly that they can see clearly where they need to search.

Never give up. Just keep your own Light shining steadily, and don't try to force change in others because it is not for you to see what this Light is accomplishing deep within the heavily fortified and camouflaged depths of other people. Allow the Angelic personnel the freedom to help, because these Radiant Ones will do whatever they can to help that golden key open the door and let in the Light. They will help the fearful ones to know that there is truly a key [symbolic or otherwise] to be found that, when turned, will release all their fears.

Never give up on a fearful person, because singly and collectively they are an integral part of a rather interesting backup plan. Of course, the words 'backup plan' is my way of explaining the huge untapped source of creative energy pounding on the door of the room that is filled with fear and addictions. The creative energy wants to go into that dark room and disperse the darkness within.

This is the end of our session today, dearest daughter.

*The above was written in the morning session that began at 8 a.m. Before the day was over, I had experienced an unexpected and coincidental connection with a stranger who came up to me out of the blue and told me she was a drug addict. This person did not like what was happening to her and begged for advice and help in understanding what was happening to her.*

*I am not a counsellor, but taking from the advice and ideas expressed by Samuel that morning, I was able to give some friendly suggestions that from my perspective were pertinent and helpful to the troubled lady.*

*The occurrence of physical examples and specific scenarios relating to what was written not long beforehand is a continuing source of amazement to me. I live in what would be classed by most people as a remote, quiet, and isolated place, yet somehow or another, the words often spring from the page and into real-life examples.*

*Since that last book dictation, this area on the North Queensland coast experienced a lightning and thunderstorm of major effectiveness and awesomeness. The countryside was already rapidly greening as a result, many of the native trees were now in bloom, and the butterflies were enjoying the smorgasbord on offer.*

*The little creepy crawlies, many who found shelter inside my flat during the storm, were now trying to find their way back to the outside greenery. It seemed a different world, where I was in that moment, to the world that was trying to survive a deep dry and depressive time not that long ago.*

*The weather is not the theme of Samuel's book, but it was something that had been affecting me in a personal way. The little flat was snuggled into the bushland, with a hill rising steeply along the eastern side of the building.*

*The following sentences are a reply of sorts, to my comments.*

Good morning, dearest daughter. I greet you lovingly this fine day. The ensuing effectiveness of the book will be as thunder and lightning. I wish to come quickly into the inner spaces of the reader's heart and drop some insights quickly and surely into their inner landscape, then depart for other realms, leaving this inner landscape to blossom with new ideas, new thoughts, and new understanding of what I have spoken about.

You may Call me Samuel, the Thunder and Lightning Prophet! Call me Samuel, the Storm Prophet! I have been called many names, and these are at least descriptive ones.

These blessed young ones will enjoy the newness of the greening. Many of these newborn creepy crawlies and beautiful, fluttering butterflies will be as one with Mother Earth because they exist in their zones, accepting totally their place in the Whole. Even newly born, they know what they need to know. They see a different world to the one you see, yet they are the same.

Remember what I have spoken about previously? I give you a gentle reminder on how you are an integral part of the Whole, and how you have the same spark of life as your creepy crawly and flitter bug friends. It is the knowing and understanding these connections that you need to remember.

Mind you, you do have a slightly different evolutionary goal than that of your little friends, but intrinsically you are all in the same pot of soup. Watch carefully how these little creatures react to weather extremes. Do they panic and get afraid and sit on a leaf that exudes a narcotic chemical compound? Do they imbibe this compound, this numbing substance so they don't need to face the reality of their situation?

No, you usually see these little ones do something instinctual and something practical; they find shelter from the storm and wait patiently for it to pass. And when the rain and thunder have stopped, they come out from their haven and go about their business.

You all have the capacity to do the same, to find shelter in the stormy times, and to thrive in the plentiful times. There are well used patterns of behaviour that will allow for empowered survival if utilised with good intent.

In this aspect, you are different to these little bugs because you also have the capacity to create patterns of fearful behaviour that will not allow you to thrive in an insightful way. It is having the knowledge this type of behavioural pattern exists within everyone, and the acknowledgement and the acceptance that everyone needs to release these patterns of disempowerment, that allows humanity to evolve into greatness.

It is the understanding and the release of these fears and restrictive behaviours that allows a fearful person to slough off the blindfolds and begin to see the magnificence of the bigger picture. This person begins to see the ramifications further than the day-to-day reactive actions, and will not only know the right action to take in any given situation but will also know what ripple effect personal actions may have on the places and people around them.

What is more, they will also know how these ripples will affect and influence future, past, and present events. Unlike the little bugs, which are always living in their Now, they live in their expanded Now.

It is all rather fun, this understanding of your actions. You can deliberately create smooth ripples, crossed and stormy ripples, sweet gentle ripples, humorous and enlightened ripples, or huge overpowering ripples.

Hey there, dear reader. You are a ripple maker of great skill and excellence. Did you know that? Shake off your fears, go out into the world, and make loving ripples because you know what ripples do, don't you? Once started, they continue and continue; they ripple around the world and sneak right up to you from behind. It just proves again the old adage:

"You reap what you sow."

Do you love the fine dust that has settled on the windowsill? Do you sweep it away without a thought of the individuality of the dust motes who reside on your sill? Sweep away because the dust motes don't mind, because they experience a continuous Now, a now without fear, without depression, and without anger. Their addiction is life being lived as fully as possible in their Now. So, sweep away, but as you sweep, think about the lack of fear these dust motes have. They have an empowering connection to their Now, and not a camouflaged or deeply hidden addiction to a fear of their Now.

Do you love the way the birds enjoy the first moments of sunshine after a storm has eased? Be as free as these beautiful ones, and shuck away any fears, and your lack of confidence and uncertainties. Look at the other side of the balance; see love, happiness, exciting expectations, and self-security. See Light and see Love, and feel at one with your Creator. Fun, isn't it?

This is the end of the chapter, and I wish you a beautiful day.

*There was a great deal of happiness, of an uplifting feeling, as this chapter was dictated. I finished dictation for the morning wanting to go out and float around with the butterflies! I didn't particularly want to dust a windowsill and check out the dust motes residing there because I really wanted to float with the butterflies, or wind surf with the birds as they gleefully embraced the power of the wind lifting up and over the line of coconut trees.*

# 15

# TIME FOR ACTION

Good day, dearest daughter. This is a spontaneous session. Just allow the pen to flow and keep the words rolling. This chapter is a short one. It is still about addictions—but addiction to life and living, not to the life of non-living.

Firstly, I say this: Despite what is being shown to you in the public media, with the concentration of resources on war and confrontational talk, and all the troubles and woes of mankind, there is an upside to your existence, and it is this you always need to be aware of and to remember in the time of troubles.

You can easily become lost in the discord and lack of peaceful unity displayed by many of your political leaders, countries, and nations. It is time for you to find your positive, life-affirming level in the personal world around you, because this empowering level is waiting for you to notice it and to interact with it.

So, look to your spiritual side. Look towards the bountiful abundance of the Great God of the Universes. Look to the Love that ties all living molecules into one huge, unlimited puddle of Love and Energy.

The Hope of all Worlds is still alive and kicking strongly. It has not been shattered and dispersed. It has not been flattened into nothingness, nor has it disappeared under the massive weight of despair. This Hope is alive and well and is imprinted in your DNA. Maybe your scientists have not been able to isolate it yet as they have done with so many other bits and pieces, but as a whole scientists know there are many things in the cellular matrix that they are still unable to identify.

The Spark of Life... the love and connection to your creative God. You know what it is. It is a drop of the Creator's Love, Hope, Energy, and Strength. How you know this is simple. You came into existence in full knowledge of this; you have always known. It is only sometimes, here and there, that this knowing has been forgotten. The blindfolds, the confining blankets, and the self-inflicted hobbles are now being loosened.

You see, it is timely now to remember fully who you really are. The Hope Within springs eternal; the way to the higher evolution of mankind is nigh. Who will not step out of the darkness of not remembering, and help the masses in the time of their direct troubles? Who will be game enough to become a Warrior of Love and Peace, a warrior who is able to show the multitudes, whatever their individual religious beliefs are, the way towards Home?

Hope is a strong, unbreakable part of your existence. You cannot lose it; it is there, always there. It has an addictive quality that empowers you in all ways. The addiction of loving Hope! If you need an addiction, this is the substance I recommend for you to try because once you open up to this energy of hope, you are drawn as a moth to the flame.

Tap into Hope, because the time of your species' survival is now coming into a critical time. How can I say this any clearer? It is time to get off your chair and do something for the betterment of all. And remember, by survival I do not mean whether the species will become extinct or not in the physical sense. I mean the chance for humanity to shine, to shine in the Light of Evolution, to shine so brightly that the next step towards Home is activated safely and well.

Become a beacon of Hope so that you help others to see that all is not doom and gloom, and so you may help others realise that they too have a big part to play in the vibrational uplifting of the Planetary Energy. And again, I remind you, the Planetary Energy includes everything animal, vegetable, and mineral. Everything and everyone.

*Hope is the Hope of good things to come.*

*Hope is the hope of all that you know.*

*Hope is the key to finding the way,*

*To Grace everlasting, to Love, and to Home.*

You may feel this is all the rantings and ravings of an old fool with all this talk about the good and the bad, and all the statements that say you are One with everything else. You may think I am this fool, but know that even a fool has hidden agendas, among them to entertain others, and to help others to let go of rigid social controls.

In a foolish way, the fool is a pathfinder into new behavioural patterns and acts as a mirror for the masses so they may see how they are behaving. A fool is only a fool in the eyes of the beholder, not to themselves. You know what I have said about living your life in a state of worry because of how others may think of you. It is not a good state of affairs when you allow others to dictate your life, especially when you are working on major personal issues.

Do you allow others to take away and deride your state of Hope? Do you allow this to happen? Be honest with your answer because the answer will only be heard by you. Do you want to continue to fool yourself?

"The Hope of Mankind" is the type of phrase that has been bandied about for ages. Have you taken a moment of your time to work out what the word 'Hope' really means? Does it mean you hope that a Saviour or Redeemer will come galloping into your life on a white horse, or will come galloping down from the clouds and save you from your sins? Tough luck if you believe this, dearest reader. It is you who have to get moving; it is only you who can change what needs to be changed in your beliefs and behaviours.

It is only once you have changed these beliefs that you can get up on your own white horse and gallop towards the total recall of whom and what you really are. For goodness sakes! Do your own redeeming. You have the ability, the self-interest, and all the needed help available to you to be able to do so. So, why wait for a mythical guardian to come and save you? Do it yourself. Many steps to help you begin this redeeming have been suggested in this wordy wonder.

A moment here, just to break the continuity of these words, I wish for you to do a small thing at this point. Put a page marker or bookmark in the page you are reading now and then shut the book. Yes, close it, and then hold the book in your hands. Close your eyes and keep them closed.

Quieten the jumping thoughts that are going around and around in your mind; let them fly out the window. After a quiet moment, while you are still holding the book in your hands, ask that when you open the book randomly, the pages will contain information that you need to read again and understand in a way that will give you a starting point in the redemption of you. Ask that the words selected will help you to prioritise what it is you need to attend to right now.

Still with your eyes closed, gently flip through the book and allow it to fall open. Without conscious control, let your fingers touch a place on either of the open pages. Leave your hand there, indicating a place in the wordage.

Now is the time to open your eyes and read the words and ideas expressed that you yourself have chosen to reread. These words will have a major clue, a signpost for you to note, and they will give ideas on how your Inner Self has suggested you can begin to help yourself.

Fun, isn't it? This is no lengthy, highbrow discussion about what to do, just a quick, intuitive helpful hint. And it took only seconds of your time to find it.

You may have heard about this exercise before; it is certainly not a new idea. Yet as simple as it sounds, the end result or the specific words you have chosen may have major insights and answers for you. Have hope. Trust that you get the helpful hints that you need to find a new sense of purpose.

So that you do not get bogged down in depressive thoughts when you think of the immensity of what you need to do personally, and what needs to be done by mankind in general, let me be quite clear. The smallest enlightened deed, thought, or belief can change the smallest emanation of the vibration of

Love into a powerhouse that can trigger a massive difference to the whole.

Begin by doing one simple task. Concentrate fully on that, and the rest of what you are trying to do will become easier and easier to accomplish. Do one thing at a time, whether it is small or large. Don't look forward along the line of what you believe will be difficult situations that you know you will eventually have to deal with. Deal with the first issue that is directly in front of you now, and by doing this you will subtlety alter the rest of the issues that are waiting in line.

If you successfully do this first task with Light and with Love, then this vibration ripples backwards and forwards along the line. When you have successfully accomplished the second task, using Love and the Light, this also ripples backwards and forwards along the line.

Therefore, it stands to reason, the further you advance along this line, the easier your tasks will be, because you have already begun the changes. Do you now see how these future changes begin from a single task well done or even from a well intended attempt in the time of right now?

Alright, enough talk. It is now up to you to open up to the Love, Light, and Hope of all the Good Things to Come. It is up to you and you alone to begin releasing unproductive beliefs and replacing them with the magical Love of your Creator.

It is up to you, with all the help you need from your friends both in the Spirit Realms and the Physical Realms, to begin your journey Home, with a new determination, a bounce in your step, and a smile on your face.

There is Hope for mankind, there is Love aplenty; there is Light to show you the way. A way towards Home.

LOVE.
LOVE WORKS.
LOVE WORKS WELL.
LOVE IS THE LIGHT.
WHAT MORE CAN I SAY?
I AM SAMUEL, AND YOU KNOW ME BY
THE NAME:
SAMUEL THE PROPHET.

# ABOUT THE AUTHOR

Helen Porteous is an Australian by birth, and had a rural upbringing that helped open up a deep love of the natural world. A prolific reader from a young age, adventure yarns and metaphysical stories were her favourite reads.

The metaphysical interest intensified during varied careers such as nursing; opal mining; natural therapies such as Applied Physiology, Crystal Therapy, Advanced Reiki; and caretaker, among others.

After a drastic medical situation, the commencement of a healing meditation regime triggered new levels of clairvoyant abilities, which eventually led to recording the communications of authors from the Spiritual Realms.